WHAT MAKES A
GOOD SCHOOL?

Tim Brighouse

Network Educational Press

Network Educational Press
PO Box 635
Stafford
ST17 0JR

First published 1991
© Network Educational Press

ISBN 85539 007 8

Books in the Teaching and Learning series designed by I.M. Powell.

Printed and bound in Great Britain by
Redwood Press Limited, Melksham, Wiltshire.

Foreword

This book is not intended for academics. It is based on years of observation and shared experience rather than research. Its intended audience is principally headteachers, aspiring headteachers, teachers, governors and parents.

I have tried to avoid jargon. Since it is not an academic book there are no footnotes but there is an appendix where those who wish to pursue the research findings further are given some starting points for their quest.

If it helps someone somewhere, not merely to improve his/her practice but to discuss it and share it with others, this book will have been worthwhile.

My thanks are due to the thousands of teachers and headteachers and other colleagues who over the last thirty years have shared their enthusiasms, thoughts,expertise and sometimes their disasters; without them it would not have been written. If I started to name schools it could be invidious: there are so many whose practices inform this book. I must, however, thank Peers School, Oxford, with whom I have parental connection and whose practices extensively inform the material in Chapter 5.

Thanks are also due already and prospectively to the teachers in schools in Manchester, Hereford and Worcester, Shropshire, Staffordshire, Gloucestershire, Newcastle-on-Tyne, Derbyshire, Hampshire and Barnsley.

Thanks finally to Joyce Randle for her unfailing sense of humour and remarkable patience, not to mention her ability to decode hieroglyphics.

Tim Brighouse

CONTENTS

INTRODUCTION

So what is a successful school? How would you recognise one? Does it necessarily have school uniform or dress and is there an honours board? Do you need to see the exam results? Or is it sporting success? And where do those excellent musical productions fit in? And if you think it is all those things, how do you recognise success in a primary school or a special school?

Is it to be affirmed or denied by the views of the people in the school's locality, the shop keepers in the town centre or the local employers? Is it to be won or lost by the messages and views of the staff who happen not to be teachers at the school - the caretaker, the secretary, the technician, the classroom assistant, the school meals staff, or the parents or governors?   Is it to be seen in the behaviour of the children?

Is there a way of comparing the success of the school in a prosperous, leafy middle class area with another school in a deprived inner city or a school in the south with one in the north?   The questions crowd in.

Unlike a company with a profit and loss account, a school's balance sheet is more difficult to read and it may not show up in any case until years later. How do you take into account events such as that raised in a recent letter from a London teacher, who writes to me from time to time:

> **One of my Year 9 girls has just started to read after six months of our mutual struggle. The moment was indescribable: she is walking on air and we have shouted our joy from the rooftops.**

Some things are clear: if 30% of the children at the age of eleven cannot read their own language, if there are pupil exclusions every week, if the staff turnover is very high, if there are fights everyday in the playground, if there is no child's work displayed in the classroom or if it has been there all the term, if the teacher cannot tell you about promising signs in the development of each and every child in their classroom, *you have got problems.*

If 80% of youngsters leave school with E, F or G grades, or none at all, if there are very few extra-curricular activities, if the library is empty of youngsters, if the musical instruments are lost or broken, if the absentee rate in the fifth year (Y11) is 50%, if there is a high incidence of staff sickness, *you have found a disaster.*   It is very short odds that the staff in such schools are miserable. Ask yourself the question whether you would send your child to either of those schools and then whether you believe that group of researchers who claim that schools don't make a difference?

This book starts from an entirely different set of assumptions. First and unequivocally, I believe from close observation over 25 years that schools do make a difference; that they can have a massive effect on children's life chances, whatever their background, for good or ill. I pity the thousands of children who go through school without experiencing a worthwhile relationship with at least *one* teacher: they have not really been at school.

Secondly the book makes the assumption that those involved in every school will want to make it a successful place; that if you scratch hard enough, all staff when they are appointed to their post in the school will reveal a *dream* or a *vision* of how things could be in their classroom and in their school. The purpose of this book is to help that vision to be realised. It is for teachers, coordinators, heads of departments, deputies, headteachers, governors and actively interested parents.

It is written as, with a group of committed colleagues, I start a research project into the issue of successful schooling in half a dozen LEAs with three times that number of volunteer schools. We shall be finding out - indeed already are - more about the subtleties of success with those participants. We hope we shall be given the skill and find the energy and inspiration to *see, record* and *disseminate* the findings, in a way that will be accessible to the thousands of those involved in schools, committed to twisting and turning their practices to *unlock the mind and open the shut chambers of the heart* of each and every youngster in their charge. Nothing less will do. We are already excited by what we find.

The book has the word 'good' in its title to quantify the school I seek to describe - yet I prefer 'successful'. Schools should be places where everyone of its community tastes the confidence which comes with success in some form or other. This book, and later the research, is devoted to the simple proposition that every youngster ought to be entitled to attend a *successful school* and that it is very much more rewarding for adults to work in a *successful school.*

I recognise above all the elusive matter of *melody* in schooling. So many people would benefit by getting to know even the words - and this book and the research will contribute to that a little - but the words without the tune would be a very lack-lustre affair. It is the *tune* we are after.

Leading to Success

An Exploration of Issues of Leadership and Management

LEADING TO SUCCESS

1) Selecting Headteachers and Leaders

The Context

"Absolutely useless" was the Education Officer's verdict. Yet at the time and since it puzzled me.

The judgement was passed on a headteacher of a school in sharp decline in reputation, in numbers - indeed in any indicator of measurable achievement. Everything told the same depressing story: the staff turnover rates had suddenly escalated so that there were either the very young who were escaping at the first opportunity or the very old waiting for early retirement. The strong mid-career head of department in the mid-30s to early 40s, who had been a feature of the school's heyday, had moved on soon after the new head had arrived. They were not replaced by the same calibre of able and heavily committed teachers who had been excellent role models, not merely for the pupils but also for the younger staff. On the contrary, the jobs had gone to poor appointments either from within or outside.

There was other corroborating evidence. The exclusion rate was going up: the Education Welfare Service was reporting an increased workload from truancy; the peripatetic musicians had fewer clients and the Divisional Officer's complaint file was beginning to bulge. The head's analysis to the governors of the exam results was beginning to vary from year to year in order to emphasise the features of success and conceal the acknowledged widening areas of failure. Staying on post-16 was steady but drop-out rates after the first year sixth told a sorry story.

The governors were collectively loyal and unquestioning but privately and individually alarmed and looking, as they always do in such circumstances, to the Authority to do something. There was no question about it - one of the Authority's more successful schools was in decline. Only the CDT department continued to shine under the leadership of a robust head of department, an engagingly self-motivated renaissance woman, with interests far beyond the school and a productivity and work rate which made mere mortals breathless.

Success in one headship is no guarantee of success in different circumstances.

And yet it puzzled me, for the headteacher had been a head before, apparently with a proven successful record, confirmed not just by the conventional referencing system but by double checks through the network of previous working connections which the Authority regularly used to vet key appointments.

It was a case study which confirmed two truths: the first, that it is impossible to have a good and successful school without a successful leader, is well known; the second less so, namely that being a successful leader *once* is no guarantee that you will be so again either in the same place or elsewhere. In unpicking this second point, it may be possible to increase the likelihood of those with the duty of *selecting* leaders and those trying desperately hard to *exercise* leadership, to do so successfully. (Nobody after all sets out or easily settles for failure.)

So what are the contextual factors affecting leadership? There are at least three: size, time and place.

Size

Running a small school or department may not help in running a large one.

It used to be thought in Oxfordshire, as in other Shire counties, that a promising young primary teacher should first serve his/her probation successfully as a headteacher of a 2, 3 or 4 teacher village school, before aspiring to one of the few larger primary schools. The policy originated in the need to revitalise the many small rural primary schools after the war when they had often been staffed for years by unqualified teachers.

It was part of the pioneering policy and practice of a down-to-earth but charismatic northerner called Edith Moorhouse who made Oxfordshire and successful primary practice synonymous. A quarter of a century on, in a less deferential and more changeable age, the policy was careworn. She, but not her successors, would have recognised the changed circumstances.

It was not merely a *logistical* issue, although there was a bit of one, since clearly if there were many more small primary schools than larger ones (which there tend to be in rural areas) it seemed inevitable that some appointed young would grow old in their proving ground! In fact the logistical issue was not really a problem because Oxfordshire's primary teachers benefited from Edith Moorhouse's success in the sense that to have served in Oxfordshire gave applicants for headship elsewhere in the country an edge, so that those who really wanted to move on to jobs with wider responsibilities could always do so if they were ambitious. No, it was more to do with the obvious point - that to run a small school was not necessarily a good or sufficient training for running a larger school.

The size and range of the relationships which have to be sustained in primary schools with 10 to 15 teachers and half as many again other staff, not to mention 300 to 400 children and their parents, is many, many times greater than in a 3 or 4 teacher primary school with 70 children and parents in a settled community where the seasons impose a rhythm of their own.

So the experience gained as deputy or in a post of responsibility in a school environment comparable to that for which a candidate is an applicant may be important. It is not that people cannot make the transition: simply that it is important that they show at interview and in practice, their realisation that leadership in a small school environment is quite different from a larger one. Clearly if there is a finite number of interest groups who have a legitimate call on the leader's time, the larger the number in any group, the more the leader needs to reflect on the best way of organising his/her time in order that each individual receives the attention he or she deserves.

The example is not confined to primary schools. To run a secondary school of 500 is a different proposition from running a school of 800 and that is different from running one with over 1200. Indeed at that point the complexity is of an order which begins to demand a subtlety of leadership skills, and a deep sensitive understanding of those issues; such qualities are rare. The jobs are simply quite different.

> A headteacher I know and admire in a three form entry school decided to transform expectations of pupils and staff, and this was a priority which admitted for him only one answer. He would take over the teaching of history himself. He burned the midnight oil, rewrote the schemes of work and allowed nothing to come between him and his teaching of the 4th and 5th year.   It paid off and was preceded by and coupled with a sharp and shared analysis of GCSE performances of the same pupils in different subjects across the whole age range. Results are improving in the wake of consistently higher expectations and to the head's relief - he harbours a refreshing sense of self-doubt - the history results have helped prove the point. The outcome has been successful.

In discussing the tactic the head acknowledged that to effect the same outcome by the same tactics in a school twice the size would not have been possible. Given the intensity of obligations in a large establishment, he would have tackled the issue differently. Interestingly - and it would be convincing to me if I were interviewing him for a post in a larger school - he showed an ability to identify a key issue and appreciate the imperative of size. As it happens this particular individual has worked in a variety of different sized schools. So of course it is with heads of departments or with those leading pastoral teams or infant or junior departments or upper or lower schools with different sized groups.

Time and place

Success in one part of the country is no guarantee of success elsewhere.

Leadership of schools today calls for similar qualities and skills as those required a generation ago: it is just that the circumstances in which they are exercised make higher demands. The 1980s were unsettled times: union power was exercised in a period of great disturbance to shared visions so that the possibility of *followership* on which leadership ultimately depends was made the more remote. The 1990s are no easier: times are more participative and disputatious than in the past but there is less certainty.

Society is more loosely coupled and assumptions about parents, staff and governors - the human context if you like - which headteachers of the '50s and '60s would have taken for granted, no longer obtain.   In short there are more factors of change within which leadership has to be exercised and the handling of change in any walk of life is a skill above all others, which leadership must show.

Some of the general factors have a sharply focused local emphasis; for example a multi-faith and faithless society, greater divisions between rich and poor, increased homelessness and a sharp increase in one parent families.   Other factors apply everywhere; the increased emphasis on rights and less on responsibility, the emphasis on parental choice and an increased application of market forces within education, together with the need to handle the huge externally imposed agenda of change. Above all leaders have to contend with the increased facility for and speed of communication which makes enormous demands on their abilities, for if communication goes wrong, the school's success soon becomes a fragile commodity.

The culture associated with particular *regions* of the country, however, is another contextual factor. A person who understands the nuances of the north-east may not have recognised a dependence on a natural affinity for the folklore of the people and their schools' traditions.   Success in one part of the country is no guarantee of success elsewhere. Similarly a leader who fails in an urban setting may not be unsuccessful in a rural one although interestingly the reverse is less likely to be true. Some headteachers who are naturally expert and proficient in taking by the scruff of the neck the school in decline and shaking it into a new sense of purpose and direction, are absolutely useless in sustaining a school already enjoying the fruits of success. Here the call is for the more subtle and exhausting skill of sustaining the highest possible rate of change and improvement without allowing it to accelerate unsustainably or drift towards complacency.

Schools are places where remembered successes and a sense of history can so easily become ancient rather than modern. Some leaders are successful in expansion but useless in contraction: others the reverse. There are separate and identifiable skills associated with the leadership and management of all these different situations. What any school needs to do is to analyse what its own situation is, so the chances of successful leadership are improved. So these are some questions for the would-be leader and for those who appoint:

- What is the size of school or department I am planning to lead?

- What experience have I had or observed in others in the exercise of leadership in schools or departments of that size?

- What are the constraints and opportunities that the school's or department's size, place, history and prospects afford?

2) Leadership and Management - the Need for a Team Approach

Leadership, management and administration

There is a world of difference between *leadership* and *management*: the first is primarily to do with planning and vision and the second with organisation and provision. They are not of course neatly discrete and they impinge one on the other. There is probably a cycle in the running of any organisation of *planning, organising, providing, maintaining, monitoring, evaluating* and further *planning*. (See diagram below.)

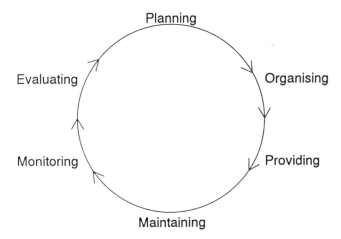

Planning

Evaluating

Organising

Monitoring

Providing

Maintaining

It is very important and a feature of long term success that the leadership of an organisation secures the effective discharge of all parts of this cycle. The smaller the institution the more it is necessary for one person to incorporate within his/her own personal functioning an ability to lead, manage and administer.   In a large and complex school, it is on the other hand crucial to know *who* is doing *what* tasks *when,* and who has *responsibility* for the tasks.

Some heads are instinctively strong on planning, monitoring and evaluating. For example they produce or enable others to produce most impressive long term development plans: in doing so they go for highly participative, collective review in order to ensure a high degree of ownership for the direction in which the school is then determined to proceed. They plan the collection of evidence and promise the review of the various new directions to which they are committed. Unfortunately they may not be so good at organising and making provision for those variables such as time, books and equipment which allow the new changes to be introduced effectively.

Others may do all of that but overlook the small detailed administrative support essential to the smooth running of any activity. The everyday back-up in the school office and technicians' workshops is crucial to curriculum and organisational change.

For other leaders, the attraction and emphases may lie differently. In a one, two or three teacher primary school, it is probably inevitable that one has to live with the combination of strengths and weaknesses which is the profile of the one individual. People outside can do their best by coaching to help their head or head of department compensate for their weaker suit but they are unlikely to do more than that.

In the medium size school - and by that I mean anything up to 1000 pupils - it should be possible for any senior management team of heads, deputies and senior colleagues to analyse honestly their complementary strengths and weaknesses and ensure that leadership, management and administration are exercised both overall and in the separate areas, for example in staff development, external relations, curriculum development, assessment systems, and so on.   It would certainly be the case that detailed leadership is exercised by different people in such different facets of school life.

When people talk about *responsibility* in the context of school life, they are usually talking about the chance to exercise leadership. For example a new member of staff may be 'taking the lead' in a curriculum development: the phrase must imply initiative and taking responsibility when things need to be done in order to see that aims are accomplished. If, however, the work they do is ignored and no one shows interest in its development, if it is *taken for granted*, the school is always in danger of slipping from a position of *positive development* to that of *systems maintenance* and to eventual decline.

The example below illustrates this.

> A main scale teacher in a small secondary school is charged with taking the lead on parents/school policy issues. She produces a report which analyses the various interactions between school and parents: *social* (PTA), *educational* (homework/reporting on children's progress), *governmental* (governing bodies/parents' educational evenings) and makes proposals for change and new developments.
>
> If the leadership of the school has not thought through the organisational ways of providing for the changes and subsequently maintaining them - or ignores the recommendations in this respect from the staff member - an enormous drain of energy and enthusiasm will occur in the interest and commitment of the staff member whose initiative is so ignored. Worse still, of course, will be the irritation to other members of staff if the initiative is improperly planned or in competition with another priority.
>
> Typically however the greater danger lies in the scheme getting off the ground and then no one from the school leadership showing sufficient or sustained interest in the tender new plant or its need both for continued but carefully measured support and appreciation and for well-timed, critical review.

What this example shows is the failure of the leaders of the school to manage the opportunity they have given another to lead properly. They have stopped short with the chance they originally gave to teachers to take a lead by not translating it from the planning phase to actual experience of leadership in action. Good management is the essential handmaiden to leadership.

Qualities of leadership - the processes in which they are exercised

Some argue that it is pointless to dwell on the qualities of leadership. *They are qualities you either possess or you do not.* The successful headteachers I have known would argue otherwise. As a young teacher brought up on Cyril Burt, I remember being shocked by Edward Boyle's introduction to the Newsom Report which argued for the first time so far as I was concerned that intelligence could be improved. But if I can accept that - which I certainly can now - surely I must find it possible to say that human qualities can be worsened or improved by the context in which they are exercised?

Leaders should never forget that they will need to deploy their own weaker skills in a crisis.

In the medium to large size school or department, headteachers would argue that teamwork can secure the complementary development of people's particular strengths. So, for example, *my* optimism can be enhanced by *your* better sense of the use of time.   Leaders get subtly steered or steer themselves into the activities they are good at but they should never forget that they will need to deploy their own personal, weaker areas from time to time in a crisis, so they need to work very hard to improve their less successful characteristics or skills. Skills of taking a meeting, of writing a paper or presenting an argument are all activities which can be improved over time.

The successful leader realises this.   Some heads do not chair important meetings or working groups but merely attend as one member, albeit acknowledged tacitly as a very important member.   Others chair all the meetings.   Some write many influential papers for those meetings, others rarely do and when they do, only on the basis of efforts drafted by others and only marginally amended.

Still on the question of context, meetings take place somewhere. But the *time* and the *place* are important. A cramped, badly ventiliated classroom at the end of a busy week, with no refreshments, where people cannot see each other, is clearly not as propitious as comfortable surroundings with a known closing time perhaps for a pre-arranged purpose involving the celebration of some staff efforts and accompanied by food and wine.

Staff meetings remain a trap for the best leaders and managers, whether departmentally or especially at school level. Once again the larger the meeting, the more hazardous the situation. Meetings too must have a purpose and their regularity should not be dictated by a calendar which is the *theft of time*, but by *necessity*.

So *every half-term, every month, every fortnight, every week, every day* are phrases which betray with an escalating sense of desperation an unconsidered use of valuable time and probably sow the seeds of irritation and exhaustion for leader and led alike. The more successful leaders have considered the following questions for meetings:

- How often are the meetings really necessary?

- Am I consulting or informing and do we all know which it is?

- Is there an agenda?

- Are participants consulted on prospective items?

- Are there sufficient items for the meeting to go ahead?

- Is the agenda circulated?

- Are items timed?

- Who is to write a brief action sheet as a follow-up?

- Are these action sheets to be made widely available?

- Who are the potential allies at the meeting and who needs to be brought into the debate?

- Who *needs* to be present and who *can* be present?

The *manager*, which must lurk under every teacher's skin, gives the most attention to all forms of communication and is keenly aware that they need analysis and evaluation from time to time. The most successful leaders change their style from time to time in the matter of communication and meetings, in order that familiarity does not dull the perceptions which they have of the school and its activities. Of course they remain constant in their *values* although they vary their *habits*.

If however there are skills which are deployed in the processes of leadership and management, they are not exercised in a mechanical or de-personalised way: to each task and activity leaders bring their own qualities, talents or intelligences. Probably of all the attributes leaders need, the ability to understand themselves, and themselves in relation to others, has never been more important.

A veteran headteacher of three jobs in three decades brought this home to me in conversation the other day, by contrasting the appropriate style of the '60s with the late '80s. Deference and hierarchy were still around in her first headship, while nowadays, although there are striking regional variations, participation and dispute are characteristics much more recognisable. Nowhere is this more testing than in the context of a school, ere is always the tension between treating children as they might become rather than as they are. A deep understanding of people is clearly desirable.

I suppose the nearest I came to affecting leadership of schools was in being involved in the appointment of school leaders, often with governors whose inexperience in the process was sometimes only surpassed by their confidence in being able *'to spot a good chap'* when they saw one.

This is not the place to dwell on the various stratagems deployed, with varying degrees of success, to overcome some of the interesting difficulties which could arise. It was always easy to convince people, however, that if there was one thing more important than an MA, a first class honours, or a PhD, worthy though they are, it was evidence of personal qualities and especially the interpersonal abilities of prospective candidates. Even the most reactionary governor will accept that. Indeed that almost brings me back to the *good chap*. What the good governors can do, as Joan Sallis says, is bring the 'bright light of ordinariness to bear': it often illuminates wonderfully.

Certainly the collective leadership of a department or a school needs to show the characteristics described below. The smaller the team the more it is necessary that many of them are present in the one person and certainly the more the leader manages to work at developing his/her own particular strengths in every regard, the more likely it is that success will follow.

They come from observations of hundreds of schools over a five year period in the mid to late 1980s.

3) Seven Qualities for Leadership

The first quality is to be *cheerful* and *optimistic*

> **Those who follow need to feel the leader has seen the other side of the mountain....the need for vision.**

This varies from simple things such as bothering to say a cheerful good morning, rather than offer a preoccupied stare, to a more considered set of strategies to find the *humour* in crisis. It is to avoid the classic story told to me by one colleague about the first day of term in a large secondary school, when the head in all seriousness said to the assembled staff, *Now I know that there is nowhere we would less like to be this morning than here.*

Even if the leader feels it - and if he or she really and regularly does, there is probably an alarm bell warning him or her that it is time to go - there is absolutely no need to mention it. One American once said that *unwarranted optimism* was the real key to leadership, and a momentary reflection of the apparently irresolvable crisis of school life confirms it.   How often has a teacher, on being told of a calamity and asked what to do, cheerfully told people to be calm and that there was no problem, when internally they were asking themselves what on earth they were to do!

Most people expect their leaders to see more of the total scene than they individually can do, so that a lack of optimism insidiously undermines their morale. In a sense leaders need vision and those who accompany them need to feel that they have seen the other side of the mountain.   If leaders are pessimistic and sad there is clearly a problem in the longer vision leaders are tacitly credited with possessing!

The second and allied quality is to be *welcoming* and ready to be *enthusiastic*

To remain seated or even to stand behind a desk which faces the door, is not welcoming to visitors. So attention to furniture helps as does the entrance to the school. The successful leader sees the need for welcome in many aspects of school life - in the room arrangement, the entrance foyer: not for them the bleak double doors with those messages to report to an office, the whereabouts of which is not immediately obvious.

It is apparent too in the processes of appointments from the interview for the new post, to a proper induction programme for all staff, not just teachers. The booklet as a guide for occasional supply teachers whose comparative views of schools in a locality can be a very telling messenger; the treatment of students in training when they are on practice, are two examples of the same thing. In any organisation the value of the smile in reception, whether from pupils as part of a rota or from staff is crucial. *Genuine enthusiasm is infectious and more than a gift.*

The head of department whose concern for optimising the style and contribution of other colleagues is evident in the welcoming of new ideas, even if some are known to be largely impractical. *We don't do things that way here* is a comment that has its place but only rarely. Newcomers can often see things which longer serving colleagues have long since ceased to notice. I admired the headteacher who asked all new members of staff to tell her after six months what were the three best features of the school and what were the three worst and why.

A third quality is the ability to be a *good listener*

It is important that when you listen to people they have your undivided attention.

This quality enables welcome and enthusiasm to be a *pastel* not a *primary* shade. Leaders remind themselves that when anyone is with them it is important that the person believes themselves to be the most important in the world at that time. Some colleagues I have known well have displayed an enviable strength in this respect - Harry Judge, formerly Principal of Banbury School, John Tomlinson, formerly Education Officer in Cheshire and the late Barry Taylor of Somerset, are three outstanding examples.

Listening skills can be improved or inhibited. For instance the clock on the wall behind the guest's chair is a temptation too much for many of us to resist. So too is the wristwatch. One of the arts of conversation of leaders is to give the impression of leisureliness even amid their frantic programme. They should be able to control its length without the sense of urgency which distracted glances inevitably convey. *I can give you five minutes* is a comment that has its place, but only rarely.

Headteachers too can ensure that there are opportunities for casual conversation: they will occur in regular, unobtrusive but natural visits to the staff room or dining area. Leaders will consider the natural habitats of their various constituents in order to supplement whatever may be the formal communication meetings in the patterns of school life. Inevitably, the teaching and other staff of the school are a very high priority so far as listening is concerned. There are many other legitimate constituents of a headteacher: the parents, the pupils themselves, the governors, the local community, the LEA's officers and advisers, not to mention the very important forum of fellow headteachers.

There is a conscious decision to be made by leaders and their colleagues in what time they intend to give formally and informally to these legitimate constituents and how collectively they intend to discharge it. The judgement of how far another member of the team will *do* as the corporate representative at a particular meeting is crucial: it will vary from time to time as well as the occasions on which more than one of the team is involved.

A fourth quality is to have a considered view and practice towards *time*

Indeed *time* is probably the key to all the other qualities. Beyond leadership and in wider aspects of the school, time is equally important. There are therefore at least two aspects: first there is time as it affects the *organisation*.......the timetable, the pattern of meetings, the rhythm of the school year; and secondly as it affects the *individual participant*.

I have already implied the importance of the choice of the representative at particular meetings in the approach to time management. I always admired the headteachers who sometimes sent a deputy to an LEA briefing meeting as much as I did those who on occasions came with their deputy. If the same head deployed both strategies I was pretty confident that at least I was in the presence of someone who had thought the issue of time through.

> I admired the principal who would arrange to meet a difficult
> parent, not in his own study but in the year head's room, thereby
> subtly implying that the year head and not the principal was the
> person who settled the issue in question. Indeed I heard tell that
> the same principal would retreat from such a meeting as the coffee
> arrived with 'Well look, you two seem to be sorting it out....I know
> you will forgive me Mrs Smith if I just leave you to finish it off. It
> *has* been good to see you, don't hesitate to let *us*' with a gesture to
> the year head 'know if we can help on a future occasion'.

If a head is always accessible, it is almost as bad as never being seen.   It really is a subtle issue. Increasingly one hears that the heads are outside school more than they are in it; it is a danger sign if that is perceived to be the case, although as the person expected to be the interpreter of the organisation to the external interest groups and so many other legitimate bodies, some time away from school is inevitable especially at a time of great change. The orchestra will continue to play without a conductor - for a while.

LEAS need to be careful not to conspire unwittingly in disabling headteachers by making too frequent calls on their time: they need particularly to counsel those heads who always appear to be a 'representative' of their fellows because they may be exhibiting signs of goal displacement. They may be running out of creative steam within their schools.

The greatest secret is to use time twice.

Perhaps the greatest secret of personal time management is to realise and then to act on the realisation that it is possible to use time twice.

Let us consider an example in the thorny issue of the head's teaching commitment. Some people say that the difference between being a manager or leader in a school and in a factory, is that whereas the latter does not depend for credibility on their skill as a lathe operator or whatever, the headteacher is expected to do the business's basic work, namely *to teach*. I know I gave the example earlier of a new head who chose to teach History in order to tackle the issue of staff expectations of pupil performance, which as it happens is an example of using time twice. Nevertheless I have been less impressed by headteachers who take on a regular teaching commitment without thinking beyond the simple motive of proving they can do it.

They inevitably do it badly since they cannot prepare so well or find it difficult to attend departmental meetings: they sometimes even find the timetable requires them to be absent at some external meeting which is totally unavoidable. Moreover in consequence, they often become bad teachers: indeed I remember one teacher saying to me plaintively that she wished 'the headteacher wouldn't teach.......we respect him anyway: he doesn't need to prove himself to us and he has got so much else to do'. It seems unlikely however that the head will entirely be convinced by that view, not least because it won't be one shared by all the staff and because of the folklore of generations.

> The head whose practice was to ask to act as supply for absences was able in consequence while teaching, to observe the marking practices and expectations of different departments: when she followed that up with a paper on cross-curricular skills and practice and produced a draft booklet for supply teachers, she demonstrated an extremely imaginative double, even triple, use of time. She is now going on with her two deputies to offer as a group to take over the teaching on two days a week for rhythms of three weeks at a time, the teaching of a subject or subjects with the expectation that the staff so released themselves observe other teachers as part of a school-wide project on what constitutes successful teaching.

Another head and a group of deputies do the same to enable departmental review and development.

Some of the questions towards the end of this chapter suggest some of the other more obvious points about time management, such as the need to have a system to ensure that all staff - teaching and non-teaching - are seen and spoken to, that double and triple bookings in one's diary are avoided, that the personal diary is large enough and not so cramped that merely to look at the daily entry is to convey subliminally a cramped and chaotic sense of stress. Routes to save time are endless. There are the familiar rules of paper management, namely not to handle some at all, some only once and just a few pieces twice. There is the need for planned free time in every fortnight and the need to ensure that rhythms are changed from time to time...the list of techniques is endless.

The major strategic decision for leaders is to try to match time to priorities and not to be shifted from them even in crisis management. I cannot however escape the view that personal time management is a key to successful leadership, albeit that the task itself is an exhausting one. I much admired one headteacher who had breakfast meetings, carefully provided in a wonderful 'Arabian Nights' domestic science room, which operated all year round as a self financing catering unit, run by one entrepreneurial staff member with pupil help. An early start was fun: it was even preceded for some by a voluntary social fitness club of staff members.

I admired almost equally another head who took off every second Monday for fishing! He was taking risks with teachers' goodwill; but each had a deep understanding of time and both with different strategies worked flat out, far beyond the ordinary, and set examples of private time too so that all colleagues knew that they didn't live to work, but they surely understood by example what it meant to be a fulfilled one hundred percent professional. Staff cars were there very early and very late and they were not always the cars of the same members of staff.

The cliche *'burning the candle at both ends but shedding a lot of light'* has at least some truth in it and it is certainly the case that teachers really respect drive, energy and commitment in their leaders.

The successful leader however does not simply dismiss time as a personal matter: they know better. The rhythm of meetings of the year as we have seen can affect success as much as the timetable. The combination of daily or twice weekly, five minute staff briefings personally attended and backed by colour coded weekly bulletins for staff information, the frequency of full staff meetings and the openness and accessibility of decision making among senior members of staff are markers of successful managerial backing: moreover they are easily analysed in any school.

At a time when communication is so easy it is extraordinarily tempting to fall into shorter time cycles for regular meetings, perhaps even compounding the problem with a proliferation of badly minuted documents on white paper. Even meetings at some schools, drawing extensively on transatlantic examples, can have an internal discipline of timed items, clear agenda and terse decision sheets, rather than exhaustive minutes.

Finally the school timetable itself makes or mars the life of the teacher and the learner by the end of the year. It is not merely the more obvious 'last lesson on Friday afternoon' or in the inflexibility of a timetable. It is in the imaginative way in which, for example, teams of teachers have time 'built-in' as a priority for curriculum development. This can be done in a variety of ways and can include the rolling programme where time is shared between staff in a way that fits the school's or department's priorities.

A fifth leadership quality is the ability to *celebrate others* and *blame themselves*

Wise new headteachers find something to celebrate in the school's past.

We all have a tendency, which needs watching, to measure the collective successful history of the organisation from the time we personally joined it. Say for example some leaders catch themselves after five years in leadership positions saying 'In the last five years we have achieved so and so': a year later it is six years! Whatever the state of the school, wise new headteachers find something to celebrate in its past: nor do they continually refer to their own previous school even if everybody silently guesses (and it would be worrying if it were not the case) that some of the new ideas came from there.

Many heads who show visitors round their schools clearly bathe in the reflected glory of brilliant teachers, imaginative and highly achieving heads of departments, inventive secretaries at the heart of the school, caretakers who do everything as well as being a caretaker and cooks who are proclaimed: 'the best in the town'. Jokingly - perhaps not accurately too - they put the few inadequacies of the place down to their own incompetence or misjudgement but always in a creative way.   Of course for leaders to take the responsibility for major errors which are not theirs, is to hold a deposit account full of credit for the inevitable rainy day when forgiveness of those who are led is required.

A sixth leadership quality is the ability to manage change

Finally, no successful leader can get very far in a school without understanding the subtlety of change in a school context. It has already been seen that teachers are experts in change, the change noticed daily in their pupils and the need to change their curriculum and their teaching methods. Kid gloves are therefore required in suggesting change to teachers in other respects.

Changes in responsibilities, while excellent for individual staff development, need to be clearly flagged if they are not to cause massive confusion amongst staff.   Changes in the relative pecking order of colleagues' pay are even more difficult, and headteachers in particular have commented about the corrosive element of dishing out 'incentive allowances' whatever the method selected for the purpose. The perception of relative merit of a member of staff among colleagues is usually very different from that of senior members of staff and therefore a decision about that person's status and salary is fraught with difficulty and danger for collective and collegiate purposes.

However it is done, whether by the head alone and furtively, or by open competition, the disappointed will see the outcome as unfair. In the late 1980s and early 1990s there has been an unprecedented amount of externally directed and sharply focused change wished on schools whether they liked it or not.   For some schools it has been a question of taking on the *National Curriculum* before *GCSE* has been consolidated: to take *records of achievement* at the same as the *TVEI* schemes: *staff appraisal* and *collective self evaluation*: *cross curricular themes* such as IT, economic and industrial awareness and environmental education.

Moreover they are doing all this as local management of schools is introduced, inducing for the leaders of the school, unless they are wary, a real risk of changing fatally their own proven and successful recipe of time given to tasks and priorities. And if the leaders are thus knocked out of their style, the rest of the staff who are used to a leader's established habits will be destabilised and left open to the fickle winds of unconsidered and ill-digested change and initiative. How on earth can the poor teacher cope with a complete change of habit in their leader and an unprecedented snow storm of change from government and LEA? Small wonder that so many complain that they have little time left to do what they most enjoy - namely teaching. By *teaching* they mean the time to prepare properly, teach sensitively, mark children's work effectivelyas well and with enough space to make proper relationships with those children with whom they best relate. The best leaders, whether of a department or a school, know this and regulate the flow of change for those for whom they feel responsible. In the jargon of the day, they conduct an *audit of change* and act accordingly. Moreover they know the subtleties of introducing change, the importance of making it fun, of knowing the first few steps in a new skill or way of doing things, the hazards of describing too greatly the extent of consequential change. They know also how carefully to orchestrate change over a period, so that people don't panic at the scope of the vision.

A seventh leadership quality is to have a clear *educational philosophy* and set a personal example

People need to know where their leaders are coming from so far as values are concerned.

So many teachers say they admire the effort, commitment and energy, the sheer hard work, openness and good intentions of leaders, where a school or department is thought successful and is brought face to face with the real importance of examples. Hard work however is only forgiven if people know where their leaders are coming from so far as values are concerned. That is probably why the researchers say that leadership is most successful after three years because until then, among other things, especially in the large institutions, it is difficult to know what makes the leader tick and therefore inevitably different decisions about personal cases will make giving the benefit of the doubt the more difficult.

There is one last point about leadership which demands notice: perhaps it is the most important of all. It has been said that the most important feature of a successful school is the number of rewarding relationships a child has with teachers: and there is much in that proposition. Certainly if a child has no meaningful relationship with any teacher, one does feel pretty sorry for them...it will be unlikely that school will have been much use to them.

> So also it is with leadership. Within the department and the school, pity the teacher who finds no one to whom they can relate with relaxation and confidence in a personal and professional way. If there were a litmus test of leadership, it would probably incorporate a way of assessing how the staff saw the trust, confidence and humour factors among the senior members of the management team of the school.

4) Some Questions for Leaders and Eight Dos and Don'ts

Of themselves and their beliefs

(1) How aware of my beliefs or value systems are the staff for whom I am responsible?

- Do they know that through papers written for staff meetings? By my comments at meetings? By what I say at assemblies?

- Am I sure my actions in respect of staff, pupils and my use of time match those beliefs?

- What actions in the last week, month, term, prove that I value individual members of staff?

(2) How far do the institution's practices, marking, awards evenings, procedures for staff appointments, reflect our collective beliefs?

Of their personal skills and competencies and their match with the institution

(3) When we last appointed a member of the team, how did we analyse the complementary qualities we needed for a successful team?

- Did we need someone strong in planning, organising, maintaining, monitoring or evaluating?

- Did we need for example one whose strengths were in *shaping* or *finishing* or what?

(4) How do I match the use of my team and other members of the team to the best match of their own strengths and to the task collectively we need to perform?

(5) How are the persons assigned particular responsibilities and tasks briefed? Are they asked to reflect on the processes they will be required to implement in order to bring the task to a successful conclusion or is it just left to chance?

Of the processes within the institution

(6) Do those with leadership roles - whether in the senior team departmentally or at main grade level - receive training appropriate to their expected role, eg. in chairing meetings, in being coordinators, in producing reports, in establishing monitoring systems, in writing letters to parents?

(7) How far can opportunities for leadership be extended?

Of time and tasks

(8) How do I ensure that I allocate time to those who need praise and reassurance or interest in what they do for the school? How much time am I spending outside the school? Does my time commitment match the priority tasks of the school?

(9) Am I visible to staff, parents and pupils and am I seen in tasks/activity which reinforces the common purpose and values we collectively wish to promote within the school?

Eight points for leaders to remember

Whether as a head of department, a main grade teacher with leadership responsibility for a particular aspect of school life or as a headteacher there are a few simple *dos* and *don'ts*. The best list I came across was in Canada prepared by a teachers' federation in conjunction with Professor Michael Fullan of the University of Toronto. He had ten points: I'm not so ambitious and will settle for eight of them:-

1 Keep it simple

So many of us over-elaborate. One teacher I knew overplanned and overmanaged so that everyone felt oppressed by long documents, complex diagrams and elaborate systems that logically should have worked well if only they had not been surrounded by human beings with all the frailty of memory, misunderstanding, and fallibilty we all bring to our daily lives. The more elaborate the planning and management the more likely it is that things will go wrong. The Canadians put it nicely when they say that "striving for complexity in the absence of action can generate more clutter than clarity".

Moreover the real sense of cameraderie and ownership always comes from shared action rather than shared planning. If you intend to have a grand vision it's best to get started in a small way with a few things. The more complex the change the more important it is that the planning and managing is loose: for to tackle it otherwise encourages dependency and diminishes the improvisation essential at the start of any important changed enterprise.

2 Avoid transferring the blame to actions beyond your control

Colleagues are often inclined to sympathise with leaders as having an impossible job. Such notions must be rigorously resisted and leaders must give the impression that anything is possible if the group are determined to do it. "If only..." is an excuse not to address an issue. It renders people powerless and inactive. The Education Act of 1988 is a reality: so is the shortage of cash: the teacher shortage or the teacher surplus. The children from the estate do come from such backgrounds and their expectations to become committed competent adults and citizens have to be raised. Leaders must convey that everything is not merely possible but likely. If we waste time lamenting the LEA's lack of direction, the parents' fecklessness, the Government's neglect or malign intent we become paralysed, reinforce dependence, and waste time in our need to give urgent attention to raising the aspirations and achievements in the next generation.

3 Concentrate on important issues like curriculum and teaching which also reinforce the professional culture of the school

Teachers nowadays say they would enjoy their job more if there were only more time for teaching. That reflects not merely their proper sense of priority but the way in which so many of the priorities signalled from outside seem to them to have little or nothing to do with their main purpose - teaching and learning with the children. One of the heads I most respect argues that curriculum change is what teachers most respond to. "Put them in teams and the outcome is magical" is how she described it. So if you do concentrate on a few things, make them as closely related to teaching and learning as possible. As for their culture, ask questions about how the conversation and surroundings of the staff room are to be made intellectually more stimulating as well as social.

4 Practise being brave

If their leader can back the decision to concentrate on a few things by publicly deciding to pass some new opportunities by, or better still to negotiate a later date for the completion of a directive, the staff feel empowered towards their common goal. If they see the leader take risks, they too will be more likely to be innovative and strong minded and clearly focused. Some of the most outstanding headteachers I have known have been very angular to the LEA. Good leaders sometimes have to take an independent stance on a matter of great public importance: they are respected for it. Nor need courage be a negative matter: it is best exercised when it is cheerful, determined, positive but definite.

5 Empower others

An acid test of leaders occurs when something is revealed to be happening which is different - indeed rather innovatively daring - even risky, but not known to them. Of course their hearts miss a beat at such moments because they are being put at risk. But the best will not say "What on earth is happening?" but "Isn't that great - how tremendous that such exciting things take place here. I must try harder to notice and congratulate good practice". Staff

need room and permission to try things out. They need also
celebratory occasions for their successes.

6 Build visions

Not only you need to have a vision. Those on the staff trying out
anything new can be encouraged to articulate their dreams of how
it will be when the dream is realised in three years' time or
however long it will be to bring the full fruition to the schemes.
The consistent use of the word "why?" can usually prod even the
least forthcoming to reveal their dreams for the sometimes small
changes they are trying to implement. From building on such
small changes and visions a department and a school can create an
ever larger shared vision.

7 Decide what not do to

So many leaders burn themselves out by trying to do everything
themselves: so many more become impotent because they do
nothing themselves. The issue of time management is crucial. It is
not *doing things right but doing the right things* as the cliche goes.
I am certain that a leader is a public and not a private person........
that it is the public occasions that take the time. Nevertheless there
is the necessity to decide what you are not doing and remember
that one rule of management is that time must be used twice.

8 Find some allies

Interdependence is crucial for the stimulation of intellectual
curiosity and the sharing of ideas. Other leaders in the system -
other departmental groups outside the school - are crucial, not least
in ensuring that innovatory practices which you wish to espouse
cannot be picked off as rogue and singular. The most exciting
innovations are always being represented as part of mainstream
thinking.

Interlude...

The Governors' Meeting

School one

Each governor entered almost furtively after a hesitant knocking, weighed down it seemed by associations of long ago. The headteacher, seated at his desk, continued his phone call: his deep baritone voice seemed to deny the necessity of a phone at all, and without a pause he gestured each arriving governor to take their allotted place at the honey coloured board room table with straight back chairs which dominated the room. A gown hung from the back of the door. As they pulled their agendas from torn brown envelopes, some whispered to each other. The Chairman bustled in, a turbulent man with a braying voice who had made his way in the world. The head completed the call: "It is County Hall again", with an expressive lift of the eyebrows. "They have not got much to do after LMS but they cannot even get the buses to arrive on time". There was a nervous rustle of laughter.

After a preliminary muttering between the head and the chair of the governors, they took their joint places at the head of the table. The agenda consisted of the Minutes of the previous meeting, the headteacher's report, matters from the DES and County Hall, AOB and the date of the next meeting. The Chair of governors welcomed 'fellow governors' and promised that refreshments would arrive in an hour and a half which "should give us enough time to get through our agenda".

The headteacher in fact conducted the meeting prompted by the occasional comment from the Chairman. The GCSE results, even at a cursory glance, showed some remarkably uneven performances between subjects (for example, 10% of the cohort getting grades A to C in Maths but 40% in English) and were rehearsed by the head as they has been for years as "the best ever in some respects". There were some questions from the parent/governor who had earlier confided her disquiet to one of her neighbours about some very bad results she had heard about. She questioned the results in History which seemed much worse than in Geography. The staff representative complained of the damage to staff morale of negative comments from governors at this difficult time. Then the governors settled to their usual comfortable hour's discussion of the shortage of cash and the state of disrepair of the existing buildings. The phrase 'opting out' was linked to the threat "unless something was done."

Staff changes showed twelve new appointments in a staff of fifty: it had not been that different in previous years. The head, who had been at the school for the last six years, thought there nothing "particularly exceptional about the turnover". Tea and biscuits arrived and the governors went their several ways.

School two

The primary school's resource and library area which links the entrance to the hall is carpeted, there is a multitude of plants and display and a draped table with its soft drinks, wines and eastern food is decorated with flowers. The open governors' meeting has been in session for an hour already and the six dispersed groups each of three or four governors, parents and staff have reconvened to share and compare on a flip chart their respective priorities for staff, parents and governors, to improve the school's practice in equal opportunity and reading.

The Chair - a man in early middle age who turns out to be a former parent - calls for the headteacher to report on Science in the early years. She in her turn invites a staff colleague who is responsible for Science throughout the school to report, and she hands round a slim leaflet she has prepared for the occasion. "We need an outside view on what we do," she concludes ten minutes later. "If the governors would agree, the colleagues I have spoken to among staff believe we should invite the advisers to visit for a day and arrange exchange visits with Abbey Road primary school on the other side of town, where we know that they are doing interesting work."

The governors of course agree but not without congratulating the member of staff not merely on her excellent presentation but also for the increased strength in Science which they could see in the school's display practice: she is also thanked for the enjoyable parents and children Science workshops on a parents' open evening.

After governor/parents/staff working groups have reported back on local management and community youth respectively, the assembled company enjoys the refreshments as they make all sorts of individual assignments and promises for forthcoming school events. They agree to meet again in the second half of term.

2

Reviewing for Success

How Collective Review Can Be A Pleasure Rather Than A Pain

REVIEWING FOR SUCCESS

Before the National Curriculum, GCSE, TVEI, and Records of Achievement, many schools shunned change of any sort.   Steady state institutions, they needed to be convinced that any innovation would not disturb the hard won intangible ethos which was frequently mentioned at speech days by head and governors and at staff meetings. To propose change in such schools was to be greeted by various objections......"we tried that in so-and-so's time and it didn't work" or "that might be all right for such-and-such a school but it would never suit us"..... or in desperation "if only we could try that but we have not really got the resources or the time".

The danger of this approach is that it fails to reflect collectively the sense of intellectual curiosity which is the hallmark of good teachers who constantly seek to ask 'why' with pupils and seize self-chosen changes in curriculum and teaching style as the means whereby they remain fresh and find the key to unlock particular children's minds.

So collective self-review would be necessary simply to reflect collectively the individual critical intellectual curiosity of each successful member of staff.

Avoid confusing the lowest common denominator of shared aims with the highest common factor of shared principle.

But it is also necessary to increase the likelihood of the highest common factor of shared values - the *collective credo* of the school. Some schools call them *principles,* others more dangerously *aims.* I say more dangerously if only because its the vogue for every school to have aims. Businesses, especially in America, and doubtless some schools now call them '*Mission Statements*'. Whatever they are called the important thing is to know that they are difficult, even impossible to live up to.   The battles in the successful school to square practice with aims, principles or policies are endless.

The most successful schools I have known appreciate the difference between the lowest common denominator set of easily agreed aims and the hammering out painfully but rewardingly of a highest common factor of principles. The wise school knows that they are principles which are very hard to live up to in the hurly burly of the school day.

One school said it stood for equality of opportunity but confused that with providing the same thing for everyone. For that school it was simply starting to understand that proposition that was the beginning of real progress towards equal opportunity. I was impressed with one school which had hammered out its principles as follows:

- firstly to treat children as they might become rather than as they are

- secondly to value all their pupils equally and intend to know them well

- thirdly to have expectation that every one of their students had the ability to walk a step or two with genius if only they could identify the talent and find the key to unlock it

- fourthly they stood for the successful education of the whole person

- fifthly they wanted to contribute to the development of mature adults for whom education was a life-long process and proposed to judge their success by their students' subsequent love of education

- lastly they promised to try to *heal* rather than increase the divisions in society. They determined, therefore, to encourage purpose, discipline, especially self-discipline, and that lively activity which breeds lively minds and good health. This last point encourages too a sense of interdependence and community.

Shared values are at the heart of any successful school. To find shared values would be enough justification for collective review. Shared values are sustained and not merely by collective review of course; they are reinforced or undermined by staffroom conversations, by remarks at parents' evenings, by the nature of school assemblies and who is present, even by the attitudes of governors - but they are helped by collective review.

For secondary schools shared values are much more difficult than for primary schools. Why should that be so?

In the first place **primary schools** are usually much smaller: so the drawing together of subtly different interpretations by staff in action of apparently agreed values is the easier.

Secondly primary school pupils are younger and are not yet adolescent: they are still near enough to the womb for neither the parent nor the teacher to want to hurry them into taking risks and trying out dangerous steps towards independence which, after all, is the necessarily worrying feature of the turbulent teenage years in secondary schools.

Finally primary schools have not had a problem with the shared value system in their view of the ability and achievement of their pupils. With the abolition of the eleven-plus the primary school could afford to spend some time on the development of art work with all sorts of materials and media because they knew that to do so was to tap a rich vein of talent in many young children, especially as it touched their affective as well as their cognitive potential. The history of the 1930s and the Child Art Movement starting with the exhibition of Cizek in Vienna and the influence of HMIs who came into contact with that movement meant that the Hadow and Plowden Reports, not to mention teacher training practices, properly set great store by the art work of young children.

Taking a generous view of talent or the definition of ability increases the likelihood of enabling each child to walk a step or two of the way with genius.

So too has it been with drama, with the development of motor skills, with music and so many other talents. Many a primary school's rites and rituals are testimony to their catholic view of human talent. Many primary teachers not merely give voice to their good intentions of finding the way to enable each child to walk a step or two of the way with genius, they actually make it happen in practice and celebrate each youngster's first steps on that journey.

It is as though Cyril Burt's legacy has been taken off their shoulders. Not for them the view that intelligence is generally inherited and fixed. Rather do they believe that it has many manifestations. They would agree with the American psychologist Howard Gardner's view that there are at least seven or more different forms of intelligence or talent and they are determined to find the key to unlock the particular ones for which each child shows an inclination whether by nature or nurture. If primary schools have been the prisoners of any particular inheritance, it is perhaps too slavish an adherence to Piaget's developmental stages: yet even here, the common sense day to day work with a class of children, almost as closely observed as thirty individual case studies, properly dispels the cobwebs of too slavish a following of any theory.

On the other hand, the **secondary school** which may *claim* to espouse equal opportunity, so often gears the timetable and the reward systems that the forms of achievement given precedence in practice are those associated with literary and scientific or logical mathematical abilities, so that banding and setting, marking systems, the announcements at assemblies, awards evenings, and written publicity, often reflect a lop-sided view of ability.

So secondary schools find it very difficult to hammer out shared values: in particular to find a way of counter balancing equal opportunity with providing the same thing for everyone, and the tension between *inclusive* and *exclusive* policies and practices. They would for example see the discontinuity of thinking which claimed a whole school policy for including children with special educational needs and a practice which saw the English Department ensuring that all children were taught together but a Maths Department in the same school which organised a remedial Maths group.

Finally any secondary school has to live with youngsters as they grow through their period of rebellion. Most schools see that as creating two problems which test to the limit their shared value system.

First there is the need to encourage independence in every youngster yet persuade (and occasionally insist!) that the same youngster belongs to a school and a wider society; that it is understood that to be a citizen is to accept collective obligations to others and behave in a cooperative and interdependent way. Schools which have sorted that one out, structure their programmes both in the timetable and through extra-curricular and whole school activity to enable every youngster to have and accept opportunities to take risks, explore and yet behave in not too 'anti-social' a fashion. They see it as important to know clearly what youngsters are doing outside school: quite apart from the interest and implied value they show the youngster in doing so, they are careful to ensure that the school complements what happens outside.

In a working class household the other day, I heard the comment "Susie Thomas gets up my nose........she is a git: the teachers make sure she is on any trip whenever there aren't enough places. It is girls like her from those sort of homes who have to go." The French exchange is another activity which needs the most careful handling if equal opportunity is not to be wishful thinking and unrelated to reality.

The successful teacher always treats children as they may become rather than as they are.

Secondly there is a double think in the matter of behaviour towards children in the classroom everyday and in every lesson. Consider:

> It is a tutor group in a morning period. Through the classroom door comes a thirteen year old pupil who shouts an obscenity at a class mate: it is not the first time this youngster from a secure background has behaved in such an antisocial fashion. The teacher decides to impose a sanction..... the detail is not important. At that moment Wayne arrives completely unaware of what has happened. Wayne behaves in an identical and similarly antisocial fashion but the teacher has a problem. She saw Wayne at the school gates desperately persuading his younger brother up the drive of the neighbouring primary school. She also knows that Wayne will earlier have already got the family up single handed because there is only the mother at home and she doesn't get in until 4.00 in the morning. Wayne will have produced whatever breakfast anybody had and managed to get himself to school just on time. The teacher also observed out of the corner of her eye that Wayne was jostled and provoked before entry to the classroom. It is a classic daily situation for any teacher.

Each teacher would solve that situation in one of a multitude of different ways according to the circumstances. Every teacher knows because daily they practise it that there must be more than one sanction for certain misbehaviours. Quietly they get on with it. They treat children so often not as they are but as they might become, and handle with extra sensitivity and care classmates who claim to expect identical treatment for similar offences. Consistency in the teacher is crucial but is not confused with uniformity of sanction and on a few rare occasions a sanction needs to be moderated by extenuating circumstances.

The thing which most often pulls schools apart is the staffs' collective difficulty in recognising that the same thing has to obtain when the youngsters are sent to the head or to another member of the 'senior management team.' Suddenly teachers expect identical and exemplary punishment of the offender, not least of course because deep down the occasion has been to the particular member of staff an unpleasant, unfulfilling incident during which subconsciously they will have felt themselves, at the very least, a bit inadequate. They quite forget their own previous practice when faced with a multitude of behaviours in the classroom.

Probably the best way of teasing these issues out is to do as many schools have done and devote an Inset day to a skilled outsider who will construct case studies which will enable groups of staff to thrash the issues out. Certainly it was one of the first actions of a headteacher I knew whose school was subsequently powerfully impressive in the confident way the staff all seemed to sing the same tune.

Another scheme which combines the teasing out of shared values with subsequent collective review is that advocated by the Bristol based development group GRIDS, which has developed staff questionnaires which involve every staff member in order to identify strengths, weaknesses, opportunities and threats. From the subsequent analysis the wise school will know which strengths not merely to preserve but also to celebrate. It can be used also to set an agenda agreed by the majority of staff faculty on which to examine and improve existing practices.

To get to shared values is the first important step: they require of course perpetual renewal, particularly through major occasions such as awards evenings and assemblies.

If you accept the need for collective review it is, like all aspects of successful schooling, an extremely subtle operation: at one level it is possible to give straightforward advice and the possible methods of carrying it out but at another that will be to mislead because it is so susceptible to subtle adjustment according to circumstances. Consider:

Case One
There arrives at a school a new headteacher where the school has been cruising steadily under the leadership of a head in post for twenty years. The staff know that they have lost the buzz of excitement that comes from doing new things save in one or two departments. The school has not renewed its shared commitment and aims but because the staff have been there some years they have the pride of recollected great achievements.

Case Two
A new headteacher arrives at a school which has undergone a three or four year period of considerable and wholesale change and upheaval in curriculum school organisation. It was not subtly arranged and many staff have been bruised in the process. The perception of the community surrounding the school is that the former headteacher had 'sorted the school out'. The needs of the school are that the momentum of change is not lost but that the

whole school commitment to the school's new direction needs to
be secured in practice rather than rhetoric.

Case Three

An existing headteacher, eight years into the job, is conscious that
shared aims, objectives and values continue to be sustained but that
the edge has gone off critical self review in some departments and
in the school as a whole, and that there is a danger of complacency.

Case Four

Some staff in a successful school approach the headteacher who
has been there for six or seven years, and themselves see the need
to try to infect other colleagues with a sense of enthusiasm for
development on a weak commitment to shared values. The head is
a secure person and receptive to the proposals.

Case Five

The government or the LEA produces a series of initiatives for
change which the headteacher wishes to use as a lever to promote a
willingness to be more self-critical in a school which has been
resistant to all change for many years.

Now there are as many possible cases again as one can easily imagine. In
each one the style of leadership and the circumstances of the school and of
the time will influence the possible means of collective review.

In the years immediately after the 1988 Education Act, the difficulties of
collective review will have been influenced massively by how well external
influences are managed by the headteacher. A huge external agenda of
change may or may not be at variance with the explicit or implicit shared
value system of the school: at the very least some analysis will be required
of the match between the school's value system and the changes being
urged on it. So too will the *pace* of the implied change, for if external
changes are embraced too enthusiastically they may overwhelm people by
the complexity and speed, even the internal inconsistency of the different
changes. Staff could become exhausted and resistant to all change. On the
other hand, parts of the external agenda of change may be just the
opportunity the leader at the school needs to start to promote a debate about
a practice which has long lain fallow and owes more to tradition than
present needs.

In considering the prospect for collective review, those willing to promote it
within the successful school will need to consider into which of the five
case studies, or their own particular one, they fall. They will need to

consider too the possible variables within each of those case studies: the style of the headteacher; the nature of the headteacher's working relationships with the deputies; the other influential characters among the staff. All need the most careful thought before collective review is started. Everyone of these should influence the speed, comprehensiveness and method to be adopted for collective review.

A headteacher-initiated collective review will typically take place in one of two contexts. The head may be new with all the advantages and disadvantages of a newcomer in a foreign land, not knowing the language, the culture and what has made it as it is. A new headteacher's actions are endlessly and minutely scrutinised by the staff. There will be among the staff some awkward characters who will seek to test the new head's expressed values against their early actions in order to find a mismatch. Because people feel there is a 'new start', the collective behaviour will be slightly different. It is more complex even than that. It is not even like teaching in the same school where even within the new class, the teacher's reputation precedes her. The headteacher *is* new, whether in the role if promoted from within or from outside: the opportunities and hazards are immense. If the headteacher decides on elaborate whole school review, it is essential to accompany it with interviews of all the staff: he or she gets to know the *characters*, the *cynics*, the *wreckers*, the *idle,* the *bullies,* those *going through the motions,* the keen *careerists,* the *idealists* and the *dependable*. The whole school review process clearly can start in better shape if you know what makes people tick since whatever happens the staff are trying to calculate and influence the agenda of change.

The new headteacher who initiates a process of collective review directly has to avoid the pitfall of *appearing* to dominate proceedings. After all, we know the common feature of staff meetings and the alarming propensity of participants to identify characteristics of the chair and exaggerate them in subsequent staffroom gossip, so that if the head chairs she needs to know that it will not be long before the staff count the amount of time she speaks and compare it unfavourably with what went before. There are two equally dangerous pitfalls at the other extreme. By not chairing or leading the meetings or the review process, the new headteacher runs the twin risks of not appearing strong or worse still not interested, and in any case of losing control of the overall direction and consistency of the real process. The last is probably more apparent than real because if the headteacher has vision he or she should, by subtle questioning and encouraging and through infectiously enthusiastic conversations, be able to stimulate a sense of vision rather than the cynical resignation among participants.

For the existing headteacher who from time to time has taken the trouble to get feedback on his or her characteristics, there are different problems; those are more to do with staff continuing to see their actions in the light of previous history rather than any new turn of direction which they may be seeking to promote.

McMahon and Bolam identify and classify at least four possible approaches to getting started on collective review in the excellent handbook of management *'A Handbook for Secondary Schools'*.

 For them the options are:

1)   Questionnaire survey of staff opinion.

2)   Structured group discussion.

3)   Interviews and appraisals with individual members of staff.

4)   Headteachers select priority areas for review.

Not only are they listed in that order but the space devoted to each of the approaches reflects perhaps their preferences based on work with a considerable number of schools over many Local Education Authorities.

The *questionnaire* is a development of the familiar GRIDS approach and is based soundly on the belief that it is important to hammer out the highest degree of shared agreement on priorities for action. So the questionnaire lists various possible management priorities for the next year or two and invites the staff to tick the relative importance they would give to each and leave room for other comments by staff, with the aim of publishing the outcome and then tackling the issues of collective review in some sort of agreed order.

The *structured group discussion* invites the staff not to use a prescriptive questionnaire but to write down their views in an open ended way. The group concerned - and clearly there is a logistical problem in doing this with a very large group of staff - is then led into a structured discussion to arrive at a common set of priorities.

The third method, *interviews and appraisal*, rehearses the need for purpose behind any initial interview of each member of staff with the aim, among other things, of interpreting the data to come up with an agreed agenda for collective review.

The fourth, *Headteacher's agenda*, is what it sounds like and suffers from all the disadvantages of perhaps not commanding the real support of staff: again McMahon and Bolam advocate that if it is to be tried then it will benefit if preceded by the use of a questionnaire to guide the headteacher's action.

There is in fact a fifth option, not covered by McMahon and Bolam, but it is the one in which most schools find themselves in the 1990s. It is the requirement from outside that the school carry out some sort of collective review.

You cannot review everything simultaneously.

The first LEA to insist on collective review of all its schools was Oxfordshire in 1979: others followed suit and in doing so left collective self review as a voluntary activity. There are however advantages in the former approach, since where collective review leading to school development plans is required of schools, the headteacher is in the enviable position of using some external agency to start the process. Although this naturally helps teamwork, it can bring with it one major hazard - a mistake which Oxfordshire certainly made - namely the belief that you can collectively review everything at once.

It is perfectly possible, indeed desirable as a first step, to review collectively all the aims, preferably the *principles* of a school. It is not possible however to review more than one or two aspects of school life simultaneously.

Many of the school development plans which have followed the 1988 Act have had an element of 'going through the motions' about them. They have not involved collective review at all. Often it has simply been the case of the headteacher, sometimes involving senior colleagues, but often not, sitting down and producing a document which has then been circulated for consultation and formally adopted to meet the deadline imposed by the LEA. The exercise may or may not have been preceded by individual departments or other parts of the school organisation being asked to write down their priorities for development which sometimes have therefore been incorporated within the school development plan.

In many cases there is the awful prospect of the same exercise being required of schools on an annual basis. For this to be bearable, schools will have to find ways of acknowledging that part of the exercise as simply a bureaucratic necessity, but using the need for it to breathe vitality into its own process of collective review. They will probably do it by adopting a pace much slower than that which is being advocated from outside. So the external agency, the LEA or central government - the Falklands factor if you like - can be used to enable internal collective solidarity of purpose.

For many schools as we can see, the 'way in' to real collective review can be other than the four options of McMahon and Bolam. Indeed it is more likely that headteachers will have the fifth external factor to aid their own process and agenda: they will of course be wise to domesticate the external enemy by establishing the views and priority of colleagues on the lines of the various strategies well rehearsed earlier.

What then can a school do to enable the process of collective review not to be simply a frustrating exercise? Make no mistake about it, the process of collective review can so easily be demoralising if it is not properly planned and implemented. There are some cardinal rules to remember.

People always judge new arrrangements by higher standards than they applied to what went before.

The first rule of collective review that needs to change in practice is that people will judge the new, unfamiliar arrangements by standards which are higher than those that they apply to the old. They will be quick to find fault. It is important to remember that 'if a thing is worth doing at all, it's worth doing badly'.......'at first!' Almost any form of human or organisational activity improves with practice. Beware of making too ambitious a claim for the proposed changes and build in a review period to 'fine-tune' the new arrangements.

The second rule of collective review is that if you associate too strongly the need for collective review with a presumed value judgement and criticism of existing practice, in which many staff have after all invested much time and energy, you will build in a wasteful time and energy trap of staff feeling resentful, whether they say so or not.

 To overcome that there are four steps to observe during the process of collective review or self-evaluation.

1) What are we trying to do, what are our aims? - the **why**.

For example we might brainstorm the aims of our reading policies and practices, decoding symbols, recognising them in groups, reading for understanding, reading for pleasure, skim reading, etc. Each school, primary and secondary, will have done this exercise because reading is vital to the confidence and survival of all pupils. The process of course will tease out differences and provide the opportunity to sort them out.

2) The second step is to chart our existing practices - the **how** in order to discharge our aims.

So in the example given the school went on to review the time they gave to the task of reading, for example whether they used reading schemes, which books they were and how they were used. They asked who was involved in the teaching of reading and whether for example the youngsters - perhaps older pupils - helped; do non-teachers get involved conceivably through 'paired reading' and how far parents are involved etc?

(It is incidentally during this second stage the impatient people get off on the wrong foot by asking not *how* we do things at present but *how well*.)

3) The third stage is to enquire of the group **what** are the practices they have experienced either in the school in the past or elsewhere in their career.

4) The fourth stage is to review the **evidence** used to chart the efficacy of the existing practices which have been outlined in the second stage.

It is usually quite difficult because we often find that the evidence we use is rather sketchy and subjective. Often discussions at this point develop into suggestions which try to extend the available forms of evidence. Very often teachers will begin to work at the possibility of acting themselves as collectors of evidence - in effect becoming researchers of a sort. They may use the presence of student teachers as an opportunity to collect extra evidence, or involve outsiders.

In my experience teachers have never failed to come up with some slight improvement and change they would like to make to their practice provided they have been given time, in well run meetings, in good surroundings with suitable opportunities for refreshments and thought for their comfort. They will also cheerfully admit to the difficulty they experience in collecting real evidence to assess their own practice.

By this method staff do not have to be threatened or diminished in their previous best efforts in order to contemplate and finally adopt change as a good idea, especially if they can see that it is likely to make the outcome of their best efforts more successful in practice.

Very sadly many initiators of change, even if they get that far, leave it there. Staff have collectively decided that change is necessary and we have made some plans. They will be useless unless somebody has pre-planned the final cardinal rule of getting started successfully on collective review.

Someone needs to know the first few steps for the new arrangement to get started successfully.

It is at this point that someone needs to know the first few important steps to take to bring the new arrangements into place. That may require the provision of *time* and *resources* in order that those involved can find out more about the proposed new ways of doing things. After all even the most modest change in teaching requires time and effort: you need to plan and organise for the new topic; the new set book; the different part of the syllabus never before attempted. It is extremely costly in time and effort. As every teacher knows, hours of preparation turn into minutes of successful teaching. Moreover if you are not prepared to do that it is best to stick to the old and trusted ways of doing things.

It is a certainty that any collective change by a group of teachers will demand someone to know what the first few steps are in order that the new arrangements can be introduced and that there is a planned provision of time and training to put them into effect. Unless such time and training is planned and organised, it really would be better not to have started just as it is in teaching. All you have done is made people lose confidence in their existing practices and have given the question of change or initiative a bad name so that it is unlikely to be attempted in the future.

In one school I know the staff talk among themselves of the senior management's *NABI* (*'Not another bloody initiative'*) *syndrome.* Of course they are probably making a slightly different point about the need to regulate the flow of initiatives and to have a sense of priorities and what can be handled at any one time. But they are also commenting about the ill-planned nature of many of the changes themselves.

If however change is planned and organised well you would hear staff expressing the unexpected confession of pleasure about something "which worked quite well really" or that was "really quite fun". Then it has been worth all the considerable effort: indeed provided the new arrangements have a time limited period for review within them, the group expectation will be towards the need for continual critical thought about what they do collectively. *The circle of review therefore needs careful oiling.* The wise leader will also seek to create a celebration of events which have been associated within the arrangements, just as he or she did during the period of collective review itself.   A new history of success is thus associated with new ways of doing things.

It would be improper to leave the issue of collective review without a word or two about *evidence.* After all there is much talk about evidence nowadays, only it flies under a different flag. We hear of performance or progress indicators. Indeed the DES have issued a circular on the topic. Probably their interest arose originally from a wish to provide parents and others with more information as a tool for increased parental choice. Increased parental choice was after all one of the main objectives of the

1988 Education Reform Act: a natural bedfellow, indeed instigator, of improved levels of educational performance. For the right wing the application of market principles to education would demand some sort of index whereby schools could be judged by the lay person comparatively.

Indeed as long ago as April 1978, the Conservative county councillors in Oxfordshire called for the publication of schools' GCSE and CSE examination results "in order that parents might make a better choice of school".

The DES circular properly acknowledged that exam results might not be a sufficient indicator of a school's success: moreover as we shall show later, when exam results are used they are extraordinarily difficult to interpret. What the circular acknowledged was the need for those with management roles in a school, whether the headteacher, head of department, governor, or for that matter externally the LEA, to have hard data which might be useful to check whether the subjective impressions of the progress of the school are borne out or not. Such evidence may have very different purposes as follows:

1) Behaviour modification
This may apply to the individual or the institution. It happens in the classroom and in the school with the behaviour of individual pupils in an obvious way, e.g. arriving punctually, being present at school, acquiring socially acceptable attitudes reflected in behaviour. It is achieved by education and training: children are encouraged to understand why certain rules and behaviour norms apply but in the last analysis they are required to comply with them. Exactly the same will also apply to the staff: they too are expected to be at lessons on time, to dress and behave appropriately, etc.

It is probably worth asking oneself, either as a headteacher or as a teacher what are the behavioural evidences we expect of the whole community: how are they best emphasised positively rather than negatively and how institutional practices may or not underpin their promotion.

2) Progress indicators
There are at least two sorts of progress indicators. Anyone embarking on a change may wish to use collective data or the observations of practitioners either within or from outside the school in order to judge what progress is being made in the process of change itself.

Take a simple example: the staff may have been asked their views on school life and priorities for review by questionnaire. Very simply the progress indicator may be as simple as the production of the questionnaire by pre-specified agreed dates. Failure to do so may invalidate the commitment to the whole process of change itself.

Keeping to the same example, the second sort of progress indicator can be illustrated, namely whether the purpose of a reform has achieved its desired outcome. Therefore the nature of the questionnaire may reveal a shift in opinion or support for a particular issue. A staff preoccupied for instance with discipline two or three years earlier may reveal in their answers to a questionnaire later, that they no longer view it as one of their main concerns. (If they do, it may be surmised that whatever the change attempted by the school, it hadn't worked!) In the matter of putting a greater emphasis on equal opportunities, the school may have a series of progress indicators that are mechanistically concerned with the timetable of implementation of a programme. One school I know had a five year programme to work first at race, secondly at gender, and thirdly at ability. Within each annual programme they had targets for six activities - curriculum, library resources, communications, assessment, school rights and employment.

In practice during the first year of the review the staff found it impossible not to look at gender as well as race, so they amended the timetable to take two years and to amend the everyday practices of the five activities during those two years by a once-only look at the issue. They left a gap of a year and they believed a fourth year could serve both as a chance to fine tune all the five activities they had reviewed, in the context of bringing into focus their third concern, namely that of 'ability' and whether they viewed that concept in a generous or a narrow way.

3)   Performance indicators
For me 'performance indicator' is a phrase which has within it the implication of comparison with other bodies trying to do the same thing.

So data such as the exam results may be used either internally to promote even better performance against previously achieved standards. For example, a reduction from 12% to 2% of the cohort at sixteen plus failing to achieve a graded result of any sort of

GCSE over five years, may be a *progress* indicator. To discover that over the same five years the national or LEA wide comparable figures reveal a reduction from 8% to 4% could be used as a *performance* indicator.

What one doesn't know is the socio-economic or other variables which affect the exam performance. That is why performance indicators used for the purpose of comparison with other institutions are so fraught with difficulty. Some people feel strongly that allowance can be made for such factors and that some sort of 'added value' set of performance indicators might be produced. Such arguments may be of interest to those outside schools but they are of less value to those inside, save as evidence of what other people can achieve. What really matters to those inside is that there is an upward spiral of achievement in whatever form that achievement takes - musical, sporting, literary, mathematical, scientific, artistic, technological and so on.

Interlude...

The Act of
Collective Worship

School one

The Honours Board was sad: it remained a perpetual reminder of the story of school life which seemed to have ended in 1966 - the year the school's status had changed. Even the curtains were a torn grey. The whistle was shrill and insistent and the man on the stage looked unfriendly and threatening. Mr Edge, the deputy in charge of boys' discipline and girls' welfare, was preparing for assembly - the act of collective worship mainly of a Christian character with which schools nowadays must begin. His demeanour was taut: his movement and voice had a staccato like quality and he behaved as an actor who had wandered off the set of a Prisoner in Cell Block H, as one of the pupils later confided to me. In my day it was Colditz. His words were few and threatening. "You over there - yes you - Silence! Gregory, stop fidgeting...... remember no chewing".

Dutifully the children assembled in the echoing hall in regimented lines, left to right, first year, second, third (Y7,8,9 as we now must call them) all the way to the fifth year. It was very crowded but there was a circle in the middle for the one disabled girl in a wheelchair. A bell shrilled and a figure in a swirling gown strode to the front. His eyes never met a child's or an adult's as we galloped through a prayer and a hymn; the staff watchfully patrolling for the tiniest sign of insubordination. And a pair of giggling fourth year girls were pulled roughshod from the throng and put to stand as giants on the left hand side among the first year. The notices were to do with collective misdemeanours and the ordeal was soon over.

I talked to some of the children, they shrugged noncommittally. "You switch off see.... I think of what I am doing in the evening after we get out of this place". "Yeah," confided a colleague, "they never tell you nothing, only bawl you out. I try to bunk off assembly - it's pathetic".

School two

At another school I visited the children were sitting cross legged on the wooden floor, chatting amiably to each other or to a member of the staff, who seemed mostly to sit on low stools at the end of each row, almost hidden under the William Morris drapes. The stage had the set of the school play and the girl I spoke to said it was "Well wicked" ....they had seen it yesterday afternoon. "You ought to go if you get the chance," her neighbour cheerfully agreed. From one of the glass doors, a woman in early middle age, with a long flowing skirt, her hair bound elegantly up at the back, emerged and the low hum evaporated as she sat half on and half off a table. She picked up a book: "The boy was almost a man. He went out for a drink, the sort of thing any of us would do......." The story wound its brief compelling way, as he lost a leg on a railway line but emerged to prove points about the occasional piece of momentary foolishness, about resilience in adversity and about service for others. There was not a wandering or abstracted eye in the place.

We then cheerfully celebrated the achievements of more than twenty youngsters. Again the eyes, the applause and the laughter were testimony to the school's values. Suddenly the woman, who turned out to be the headteacher, clapped her hands "We must go about our business now......thank you for listening so attentively and for joining in the celebration of some of our community's achievements". She was gone and the low chatter resumed as the children good-naturedly departed.

Afterwards the two youngsters who had enthused about the school play were debating the story of the unfortunate young man who had been the subject of the head's story. They also told me about the two other people, the deputies, who between them took the whole school and lower school assemblies on Tuesdays and Thursdays. The other days they thought were better: "You see we do assemblies as a class or as a year - it is better when we do it ourselves".

School three

Yet a third school was a residential community of 300 or so youngsters.
To my amazement there was no bell, just a converging from all parts of the
community, with all members of the community, to a hall where all sat on
chairs in an almost enclosed circle. The headteacher, a grey haired man, sat
at one edge of the circle. We sat in silence for a while. A child spoke of
events on the other side of the world and we fell silent again.

After a while the headteacher moved and got to his feet. The school did
the same. A first former confided to me that during the assembly he was
wondering how the weather would bear up for his cricket match that night.
A child of thirteen I spoke to said he had used the time to revise in his head
for a test that day: another of 16 smiled quietly and said you thought of a
great deal of matters at that time in the comfort of others doing the same.

The first school talked to me a great deal about discipline and about
children not being how they used to be but that there was not much you
could expect from children from such backgrounds.

The second school showed me its assembly documentation shared with all
staff and how there was room for the unexpected within their plan for the
year.

The third school talked of its foundation and its beliefs.

The first two schools are within half a mile of each other in the inner city
and the third school takes mainly children from disadvantaged areas and
specialises in learning difficulties.

3

Creating a Successful Climate

The Importance of the Visual, Aural and Personal Environment

CREATING A SUCCESSFUL CLIMATE

'Surround them with things that are noble'. A great Victorian said it all.......well almost all, because he probably was thinking of the visual and physical environments.

Successful schools know there is even more to it than that and are conscious of the aural and spiritual environment; but so many secondary schools apparently regard the schools' surroundings as a distant after thought and certainly do not give them the attention they deserve. In doing so they leave their school with at least a running sore.

Moreover the natural inheritance, especially for teachers in secondary schools in the inner cities, is little short of horrendous. If they escaped the flimsy system buildings of the 1960s they were probably constructed of disease ridden concrete. Their windows will have been replaced as often as their flat roofs. So many also find their wiring and plumbing require renewal, disfiguring over and over again the daily environment of the teachers and youngsters who pass each other in corridors where the frequently replaced cheap tiles have made the floor an unappealing patchwork quilt. Of course all schools receive different legacies from their Authority's architects who originally designed them and those who have since sought to maintain them.

Consider the best of the independent sector. Children who attend Eton and Harrow are usually themselves from homes with fine surroundings - not just architecturally - they are probably immersed in books and musical experiences from their first waking moments.

Some of the state sector can compare. I always thought that the legacy of Albert Smith, the architect of the old Oxfordshire and his mentor and counterpart in Buckinghamshire, Fred Pooley, would stand the test of time rather better than their counterparts in some of the other home counties. On the whole the rural inheritance of the Midlands and the North has bequeathed some splendid schools which would appear to have inhabited their surroundings for centuries. To make my point I describe two Oxfordshire schools in the blanket making town of Witney, just on the edge of the Cotswolds.

One school, Henry Box, is close to a beautiful church at the end of the green surrounded by mediaeval houses. The school is a combination of the 17th, 18th and 20th centuries. There are some buildings from the 1930s and a substantial extension from the '60s and '70s. The buildings are well spaced out and close to a tree-lined extensive field. The school's inheritance would touch even the least visually aware child at some time during their career.

Wood Green is at the other end of town, a low flat, grey, concrete slabbed building of the 1950s with later additions on the edge of a windswept green field. I always found it infinitely drab. As it happens a talented Art teacher, ably assisted by a succession of perceptive leaders and committed colleagues was only too keenly aware of this. The corridors were soon the subject of a year round set of exhibitions and display. Both schools are reasonably successful but Wood Green achieved this despite a huge architectural handicap.

Why is it that children from the poorest backgrounds are given the worst surroundings? It used not to be so: the great late Victorian schools and those before the second world war, even afterwards, appeared to their contemporaries fine places and even in the '50s when the inner city dwellers were moved to new estates, the general public called their new schools 'glass palaces'. The rot, often literally, set in during the '70s in the wake of the oil crisis. Just at the time we became more generally aware of our environment and of the need to preserve and conserve we no longer needed new schools. And when schools were considered for closure as a result of falling rolls, the environmental factor had the least impact in a set of emotional and political considerations.

For most of us the 'built environment' is an issue awakened by a chance encounter often in our teenage years or early twenties. For me it was first a lecture about the 'built environment' of my not very distinguished home town when seventeen. It was as though a whole new world was open to my hitherto unseeing eyes. Later in my late twenties, a set of talented architects in Buckinghamshire opened my eyes still further to what school buildings might be like. I was privileged to take part in their critical debate of each other's designs and built results.

The playground is the natural habitat of bullies......make it a pleasant place to be.

Beyond question and especially in the desolate, grey, littered, graffitied inner cities, someone needs to make a start on improving the surroundings in which our future citizens are prepared for their future life. It cannot be right to have the school as a prime example of neglected harsh squalor. But what can you do if you happen to inherit or already be teaching in such a place? One school I know turned the vast expanse of tarmacadam into a series of different leisure areas. Let me explain.

The playground is of course the natural habitat of bullies: it is here they peddle their destructive trade among their peer group and younger pupils. Playground bullying has many manifestations: probably the most conducive to bullying is a totally tarmacadamed playground where there is much noise and unrestricted opportunity for macho sports games and imitated TV violence. It doesn't take much to break that up: seats, a few trees, some created gardens, a place for livestock, a chequerboard garden, even a pool. Clearly some but not all of the suggestions are impractical and I am here talking of a primary school example. Nevertheless the most impractical and dangerous course for a school wishing to be successful is to leave the outside environment to fend for itself. All surroundings of a school need areas for calm, for social chatter, for ball games and for the natural environment, preferably including livestock.

Buildings.......even the most drab can be transformed by creepers, climbers and shrubs.

As for the architecture of the building itself I shall never forget County Hall in Aylesbury, nicknamed affectionately after the county architect *Pooley's Folly*. The architecture, if you'd seen it, puts one in mind of a modern equivalent of a mediaeval cathedral: tall and dominating in an otherwise flat environment. The problem with the building lies in the unremittingly grey concrete. There grows from the bottom however a plethora of despairing ivy and shrubs, desperately climbing towards the fourteenth floor. It is ironic because Pooley deserves to be remembered for spawning a talented team of school architects who rejected both the concrete vogue and the flimsy system buildings, both of which were to prove expensive on the pocket and the spirit. They preferred old stock brick buildings with traditionally sloping roofs, carefully suited to school surroundings. Pooley's Folly however shows how even when mistakes are made, the nature allies of shrubs, creepers and climbers can dress mutton up as lamb.

At the system wide level, not only architects have influenced the inheritance of future generations. Henry Morris in Cambridgeshire enlisted Walter Gropius and other distinguished architects for his village colleges. Stewart Mason, one of his disciples, and later Chief Education Officer for Leicestershire, would insist as did his successor Andrew Fairbairn, that in each new school somewhere on its wall there would be a piece of imperishable prose or poetry to catch the passing pupil.

Ask anybody who attended the Barclay School, Stevenage, and as like as not they will tell you of the amazing figure sculpted by Henry Moore which simply cries out to be touched.

Case Study 1

The new headteacher of a school in a market town recognised immediately the subconscious influence of the monstrous design of the main building which people had lived with for twenty years. His first action was to plant climbers and creepers. His second was to pester the Authority for the replacement of a flotilla of wooden hutted buildings in the hope of a new block whose design might, with a bit of luck, have encouraged our architect to do something to improve the impact of the original building. For a whole generation of children at that school, the built environment suddenly became alive as the whole school community devoted their attention to the school building project as it was designed and the whole environment improved.

Case Study 2

The headteacher of the two hundred place primary school had been unhappy for two or three years with the generous, indeed over large playing fields. She persuaded the grounds maintenance team that their work would be less if half the field were left as a wild area. A goat was soon tethered in another part of the field and a dovecote appeared. Before long there were chicken and rabbit hutches and the whole community took their turn in looking after the animal community. The children of course gained personal comfort from the animals and learned a lot about the cycle of life and the habits of various species. For some of it was the start of a life long interest, for others a memorable interlude. In that school there really was no bullying.

Case Study 3

Mrs Bennett has been headteacher of a large primary school in the six towns of Stoke-on-Trent for twenty years. She has a three hundred year old hedge which bisects the site: she has enriched the habitat over the period with a wide variety of trees and shrubs. There is a long established pond which seems to predate the 1950s building but is in fact the culmination of a dozen years of whole school involvement. She confesses that part of her criteria for selection of candidates for any school appointment is their evident interest in the outside environment.

Inside the school the visual environment is equally important. On that primary schools have taught us much too. For them it probably all started with the Cizec exhibition of children's art in Vienna in the 1930s, an event attended by a cluster of imaginative and influential HMI led by John

Blackie, who was later to be Senior Chief Primary Inspector. He recruited to his ranks the likes of Robin Tanner, a great artist in his own right as well as a teacher.

There emerged a group of primary practitioners who were deeply convinced that artistic expression represented a rich vein of children's talent which could be tapped very early when inhibition was less intrusive. On the child's confidence through the successful use of various media, in artistic form, could be built success in the other talents such as reading and writing which our schooling system naturally emphasises. There is much in the argument, even if the release of artistic achievement at a young age often flatters to deceive so far as the talent is concerned. Nevertheless what emerged was a few generations of primary teachers who gave ample rein to artistic expression. Through their training and their practice they learnt the skills and techniques of good display.

It has become the rule therefore rather than the exception that the primary classroom and school itself has become a visual delight, often obscure in its purpose, and any secondary colleagues and a wider public tend to use the pejorative term 'decoration'. Yet look beyond the camouflage of the primary school and you can see its skills. For example the entrance foyer will illustrate various themes of the school curriculum or community activity. There will be evidence of practice in various media. In individual classrooms, it is as well to notice whether all the children's work is displayed.

Moreover, has it avoided the trap of those early artistic enthusiasts of celebrating only art and literary forms? Is there a mathematics puzzle or two? What of scientific work? And the successful primary school will occasionally turn the whole school display activity for half a term to a linked theme which supports a planned set of explorations or values of the whole school or community.

In the individual primary school classroom the environment is planned to encourage the child to autonomous learning: the child is urged to know where material, equipment and other learning resources are kept and to take responsibility not only individually in their use but collectively in their organisation and conservation. You will come across groups of children debating the work exhibited and visiting parents will proudly be shown their and their friends' efforts. Sometimes in the best reception and infant classrooms, the whole room will be transformed with huge models to some strange and exhilarating exhibit which reinforces the children's learning from a visit. I remember entering a classroom which was a local coalmine, another a farm and yet another a theme park.

In the best run **primary schools**, the school as a whole is a reflection of the individual classroom, larger but gaining in the process.

At **secondary schools** such individual and whole school individual environmental policies are the exception rather than the rule. Why is that? First the primary teacher, through the Cizec - Blackie tradition, has been initiated into the importance of the visual in training and almost all primary teachers have had longer training on average than their secondary colleagues. Most of them, with the exception of some in the expressive arts, have experienced hardly more than a passing mention of the techniques of display in their training. Secondly of course, subject specialisms with their deep knowledge bias demand so much time and attention that the more general whole school issues get lost. Moreover secondary heads have for years come from that tradition, oblivious of their surroundings, as their studies so often testify.

It is for example still sadly rare to find the secondary headteacher's study wall deliberately exhibiting, on a rolling basis, examples of childrens' work: and where it happens it will so often be just art. I say 'just art' not because that is unimportant but because it shows that the head has not taken on board the much wider message of the question of display.

I came across a head two years ago who wistfully confessed he knew display was a really important whole school issue but that after an initial push on his arrival it had deteriorated to almost its previous nonexistent level. I confessed I had noticed. He knew he had made the cardinal error of apportioning the job as one of two 'whole school' responsibilities, to someone who had no credibility in the staffroom. Had a document been produced to explain the rationale for display? "No!" Was the responsible member of staff initially invited to come up with short and medium term goals for display in certain areas of the school with criteria to guide choice? "Well not really". The questions and answers could have gone on: the real issue at stake however was not a judgemental review but a joint determination promoted by the head to revive the question of display. The head in question soon came up with the answer: he arranged for some of his staff from the English department to get together with local partner primary schools, all staffed by teachers skilled in display. In the second half of the summer term the best of the fourth year junior work was jointly planned and displayed throughout the whole department, so that all the children in September could see something familiar.

He did not stop there; he used some teacher supply time to promote a debate about the quality of the English work before, during and after transition, with secondary colleagues having the pleasure of sharing their expertise and skills with primary teachers in the mysteries of moderation. The next year the head managed to do the same for Maths and found his English colleagues achieved the same outcome anyway.

In the meantime two members of the English Department had become skilled in display and an Inset day was planned run entirely in-house by teachers who were known and respected as good teachers: they promoted more widely the issues of simple display, with a tactically chosen art colleague providing a workshop for staff members interested in becoming potters. Interestingly they run that in their evenings. The outcome of the day therefore was a staff leisure pottery club and a determination to mount a joint staff/pupil display of their wares in the hall before Christmas.

The illustration tells not of the answer but of one which suited that head at that time with the staff he led. He seized on something - primary/secondary transition - which was on the agenda anyway and simply fed in an idea to a group of enthusiasts. It has taken two years to get halfway there but already the school's environment is transformed for the better. I take no bets on where it will all end.

In another secondary school, four years ago, an incoming head transformed a desert of an entrance hall single-handed on a weekend, with a couple of cheerful staff volunteers: the children now gain experience in receiving visitors - a job strategically chosen for the third year. After all if any one group of children are at risk of losing motivation it is Year 9 as we must now learn to call them. They look after all the telephones too: it is all part of a carefully structured curriculum in Year 9 designed to find ways of capitalising on their achievements, and part of an intensive review of their strengths and weaknesses with extra teaching available to get them ready for the two years running up to GCSEs. I digress.

The same headteacher, a woman (it is significant that most visually aware heads I know in secondary schools tend to be women) soon tackled the visual environment systematically because she had that in mind - I suspect among a lot of other things - in the individual, informal 'get-to-know-you' discussions which are a feature of all new headteachers in their first year.

From that she found she had a team of six members of staff across all departments except Science, who had expressed keen interest in matters connected with environmental display or environmental teaching. Moreover a cursory check of classrooms bore out their practice. She invited them in for a chat one tea time and talked to them first of their individual visions and then skilfully of what emerged as their collective vision but was, I suspect, hers all along. She promised to speak to the heads of faculties concerned who were only too pleased to let their enthusiastic colleagues spread illustrations of their skills to the common areas of the faculties.

Already I have missed a step in the story - the Science department. It was agreed that the probationary Science teacher should be invited to be involved because there was no obvious person among the other members of staff. She was provided with extra Inset on the issue - as it happens from her partner who was a primary trained teacher in a nearby school. The Science team chose the topic for display and the probationer along with some student teachers at the school mounted it.

That is how it all started. Now four years on the school has children's work expertly displayed on three half terms in the year. They have considered the check list of questions set out towards the end of this chapter. Now all the staff - well all but six old reprobates who claim they cannot learn new tricks but are being increasingly joked out of it - are involved in an end of session review of the work displayed.

I should add that the six reprobates are now constituted as a panel who give an award to each department's efforts and explain the criteria they have used for the award. It was all jokey stuff at first but it is not entirely that now.

The examples of a *way-in* to this much neglected issue are legion.

That is less than half the environmental story.

What of the *'aural'*? Somebody once said that with the echoing footsteps in the corridor, the shrill bells and the clanging doors, secondary schools can be confused with only one other sort of institution. Indeed at the end of a school year the cumulative effect of thousands of scraping chairs on hard floors, of dumped satchels, of banging doors and of lesson change bells takes its toll on even the calmest teacher's patience.

When in about 1971 I first met Geoff Cooksey who was to become the inspirational founding father of Stantonbury in Milton Keynes, I could not understand his preoccupation with carpets. Let me explain. At the time I was an assistant education officer with Buckinghamshire. Among my duties was the design brief to architects for new schools and the liaison with a Supplies Officer colleague in the furnishing of them. Geoff Cooksey in Stantonbury presented an interesting challenge. I was firmly convinced that schools should be flexibly designed to encourage team work but planned in a way that allowed quiet and individual teaching and learning. It seemed to me then - indeed it still does - a pity if the building is inflexibly constructed *requiring* ,through bricks and mortar, work either as isolates or as teams. Very few architects have cracked that problem. At Stantonbury it was not such a problem because Roy Harding, the CEO at the time, recruited Geoff Cooksey from the Schools Council. He was unequivocally committed to team work and was also a charming, persuasive realist.

What he wanted however was *carpets.*

This was 1971 remember, when we had just persuaded councillors that it was not a waste of money to supply carpet to quiet areas between pairs of primary classrooms and when the technology of industrially used carpets was in its infancy. Geoff wanted carpets everywhere. He got them in most places too, and I made a hasty exit to my next job.

I remember Geoff saying once that the one simple act which could improve education in all secondary schools would be to carpet everywhere. Nowadays that is a commonplace request of secondary heads - indeed they are using any early discretion of expenditure under Local Management of Schools to carpet whole suites of rooms. One of the new London Boroughs, Islington, on the break up of the LEA, made a public priority of its determination to carpet all its schools. That it drew approving notice rather than public ridicule is a welcome sign of changed attitudes to the school environment.

The cleverer of the headteachers incidentally are linking the advent of carpets as a way-in on display in the particular departments affected by the carpeting. One of the unremarked benefits of Local Management of Schools indeed is the feeling of power schools will enjoy over their learning environment. They will no longer feel guilty about leaving the decoration to an uncaring Authority but realise that it is their own priority.

So carpets are a contribution towards an aural strategy for a school and a powerful aid to better teacher/pupil relations and more effective learning and teaching.

What are the others?

I went into a Leicestershire school one wet lunch time and couldn't believe my eyes and ears. There at the milling area, close to the entrance, the dining hall and the two main corridors, was a chamber orchestra running through their pieces. Half the dinner queue was watching and listening as though this was quite the most normal thing in the world. I asked one of the queue if indeed this often happened. "Yes," he said "but I prefer the jazz days - that's Thursdays." He was immediately involved in argument with another person in the queue who preferred the 'Asian Days'. I didn't let it drop and asked a simple question: "Who are they?" to which I got a simple reply....."Jason, Wayne, Cheryl, Sue, Brian and John"!

I discovered a pretty pleased headteacher soon afterwards who explained how the new Head of Music had decided that one way of unlocking the considerable musical interests of most youngsters was to change their environment. So for six weeks each term during lunch break the youngsters put on programmes of music which dominated the aural impression of the school's internal environment. The contrast in the other weeks was so stark that by popular request of the School Council, the music teacher arranged for each form to play programmes of request in the same area - sufficiently moderated of course on the volume key not to become a nightmare.

Interestingly the same school was debating the abolition of the electric bell system: they found it intrusive and were replacing it with a system of 'pagers' for teachers' pockets which were programmed to bleep for lesson change time.

I must say that I was less convinced by that one, but couldn't help sympathising with the underlying motive.

The environment of course is more than the aural or the visual. It is caught in the corridors, in the way people behave one to another, in doors which are held open or closed carelessly in your face, in adults and members of staff who have the time for a snatched smile or chat with passing youngsters or pass unblinking or unrecognising a fellow member of the community. How do schools establish that?

It comes from shared values, as a common agreement among teaching and non-teaching staff to concentrate on a few things and reinforce them come hell and high water. Mostly those things will be positive. They will affect the corridor and playground behaviour, the choice of prefects and their role (or the decision to have no prefects), the place for collective competition between groups rather than individuals and the celebration and honouring of excellence over a wide range of human talents. It will involve a close consideration of the service given by all members of the community, either within or to a wider community.

What few things a school says are important to youngsters carry little weight if the staff's actions and everyday habits contradict them. So the school which is concerned about the elusive third dimension of the successful school's environment will examine carefully the messages conveyed by its rites, rituals and whole school organisation and practice. Some of the rites and rituals are illustrated in the stories of school life which punctuate the main chapters of this book and some of the organisations and practices in the sections on leadership and maintaining success.

Some questions for those who would improve school climate

Visual

1) Who is responsible for display in the school and who else is involved?

2) Do the pupils themselves have some responsibility in selecting and helping the display in communal areas?

3) Have we used 'artists in residence' perhaps from the local community or through the Arts Council to engage youngsters in creating and celebrating something of beauty? e.g. sculptures, murals, other art works.

4) In secondary schools (where it is unlikely that more than a small proportion of staff have had training in display) how do new members of staff gain training in display as part of their induction?

5) When did we last use part of an Inset day to debate the visual impact of the school? How did we prepare for it? Did we use an outside or inside consultant to lead discussion within departments about display?

6) Within the classroom what are the walls used for? Are they used to display all the children's work? Are there some puzzles on the wall? How frequently are the displays changed? Is there some unfinished work to debate? In the secondary school does it reinforce the love of subject? Is it sometimes - say one half term in two years - part of a deliberately planned whole school cross-curricular survey? In the primary school does part of the work reinforce the school's language, maths and science policies as well as perhaps the topic/theme of a group of classes?

7) Outside the school who is responsible for the cultivated areas? How do we involve the older generation of the community in the maintenance and development of a part of the outside school? If our school is one sea of tarmacadam, how do we break that up? Are there seats for youngsters, especially those not wishing to be swept along in informal team games at break time? Do the midday supervisors know and contribute to the development of the external environment? What 'Inset' do we arrange for them?

8) In the professional areas, are the notices cynical or humorous? Are there photocopied articles of interest on the notice board?

9) If our buildings are unremittingly unattractive, what simply can be done about it?   Can the school be camouflaged by fast growing creepers that don't damage the fabric? What is our strategy for ensuring that we don't become or remain the victims of vandalism?

Aural

10) Are the corridors, even when empty, noisy? If so what is the strategy for changing that? How much of the school is carpeted? What are the acoustics of the hall and dining area? What simple steps can be taken to make them better - could, for example, the use of display materials help acoustically?

11) Is there a tannoy system in the school? If so is it needed? Is the internal telephone bell intrusive to lessons and what other matters can be changed to decrease staff stress? What about the tables and chairs? Do doors naturally slam?

12) Is there a thought-out policy of music for dinner times and for the social areas for breaks before and after school? Is there a mix of pop, jazz, reggae, eastern and western classical music? Is some of it youngster performed and some reproduced?   If there needs to be a bell to summon youngsters from the field, does it need to be institutional?

Personal

13) Is there a code of conduct which applies to all members of the school community - youngsters, staff, parents, governors? (See Chapter 5)

14) How do our rites and rituals reflect that code of conduct and the school's statement of principles?

15) In what ways do we collect evidence with which we can review as objectively as possible the successes and shortfalls in personal standards of behaviour within the school community?

Interlude...

The Lunch Hour

School one

The playground is tarmacadam, one unbroken dark sea with not a tree or seat in sight. A chilling breeze becomes a freezing gale in the wind tunnel between the Art Block and the main building. The school doors would slam if they were not locked and the street wise pupils know the least freezing nooks and crannies and huddle there in misty warmth.

The boys in their black blazers engage in imitation games of TV cops serials: violence is never far from the surface. Thirteen year olds are playing a huge game of football with Tesco bags for goal posts and towards the corners a knot of fourteen year old girls are loudly stalking a pair of more timid young women: in an external lobby close to the entrance, another larger and louder group conceals smokers. Conversations are about "missions" but no adult hears or understands. Around the end of one building comes a slovenly woman in a dishevelled overcoat with a cigarette in her mouth: she is pushing another pair of boys who accuse the "dinner lady" of being "a blankety blank slag". They are told not to use "them foul words on me".

Inside there is a snooker table in the almost deserted staff room where the "regulars" - the Head of History and the second in the CDT Department - are punctuating their game with a discussion of last week's football matches and the doubtful sexual proclivities of some of the pupils. In the sports hall four other colleagues are completing another round of the staff badminton competition. All is almost quiet in the school save for the dining room where the noise level is at a crescendo and stressed dinner ladies seem to show in their faces a desperate hope that the ordeal will soon be over without actual violence. A well aimed missile made out of fish-cake dashes the hope........ a shrill whistle blows and the deputy head thunders his invective at the suddenly quiet throng.

School two

In another school not half a mile away, there are tables and chairs around the trees to break up the playground. At one end a small group are kicking balls against the various patterns painted on the games wall and the headteacher, a woman in a long smart dress, is talking easily to a group of boys who are playing petanque. Inside there is scarcely a room unoccupied. Chess, electronics, railways, bridge and archaeology vie for the attention of teachers and pupils alike. There is a book stall run by a group of fifth years. A group of thirty chat to each other in the assembly hall as they watch a rehearsal for the school's production of "Smike".

Those who have chosen the school lunch are seated in the brightly coloured "all in one" tables and chairs that they themselves set out and replace: they listen to a "student's choice" jazz selection and talk, sometimes noisily, with each other and the adult member of the community who sits at each table. One set of six tables is occupied by senior citizens who take their "meals on wheels" secure in the company of the young who serve at table.

In the sports hall there are six table tennis tables set out for the upper school league: there are twelve clubs in the local league and outside netball teams are similarly engaged in serious practice observed by lots of other youngsters pressed against the chain link fence. A staff tennis match draws an admiring crowd and pupils wearing prefects' badges walk with the dinner ladies.

4

Staff who are Committed to Success

Staff Needs and Aspirations and How to Create and Maintain Motivation

STAFF WHO ARE COMMITTED TO SUCCESS

Staff Development ....leading to successful teaching and learning.

When we talk of school staff or the staffroom we automatically bring to our minds teachers. It is arguable that some of the most vital members of the staff at a school are not teachers at all: many teachers have wryly commented "if you really want to find out what is happening in the school it is best to ask the caretaker or the school secretary". And the comment, which at face value is about communication systems, conceals a more fundamental point.   After all, the business of the school - whether it concerns problem children, awkward visitors, the administrative support system, the arrangement for trips, meals, ordering equipment and supplies, dealings with County Hall, the diocesan authorities or the DES, even the governors' meetings - all tends to go through the office. Indeed if headteachers knew as much about the detail of the school as the secretary/administrator/bursar, they would not be doing their job properly.

And while on the subject of non-teachers, what of the recently acquired midday supervisors? There is little doubt that their skill coupled with the impact of the external environment at lunch times, has a profound effect on the incidence of bullying in particular and the behaviour of the school in general.   So the wise school gives a high priority to the development of midday supervisors' skills and attitudes.

So if the teachers are the people who mainly contribute to a school's main business - namely unlocking the talent of future generations - it is wise not to forget that the non-teaching staff have the potential to contribute significantly to that task. Nor is the contribution exclusively behind the scenes. How children are treated in the school's office, how the non-teachers talk to children in the corridor or on the way to school, how they deal with confidences, all affect children's life chances. What is more, as it is almost always the case that more of such staff than teachers live in the locality, their messages to the local community about what is really happening in the school are crucial. If what follows therefore has teachers mainly in mind, it is because their morale is more vulnerable. At every stage however it is necessary to stop and ask whether the same issues affect all members of staff.

Teachers get exhausted where the rest of us merely tire.

Teachers know that the inflection of their voice, the movement of an eyebrow and their attitude every minute of every day when they are with the children, affects those children's ability to learn. And they are in contact with children a lot. So it is that teachers get exhausted where the rest of us simply tire. Learning is the whole business of the school: it deserves to be in the forefront of the minds and conversations of all in school who nowadays need to guard against displacing learning by managerial or organisational topics such as 'resource management', 'external relations' and so on.

Unlike teachers, the rest of us, including headteachers, enjoy 'down time' when we are properly involved in activities which do not require us to give of ourselves perpetually: we can work in private.

All staff require four conditions to be satisfied if they are going to carry out their duties effectively. They need:

- ☐ responsibility
- ☐ permitting circumstances
- ☐ new experiences
- ☐ respect and recognition.

Let me unpick each.

Responsibility

Most people confuse *responsibility* with work. We quite like the former but are liable to get stressed by too much of the latter. Most of us, with the increased pace of communication, particularly in written form and with the expansion of knowledge, are not short of work. Indeed from time to time all of us feel helpless about the things we should have read but haven't. It is particularly difficult for subject teacher specialists, for they have seen their own field of specialism transform itself within a very short space of time - a year or two often. Publications have proliferated to an extent that it is virtually impossible for a serious scholar to be aware of the contents and impact of all that has been written in his or her subject. This point was brought home vividly on a recent Radio 4 programme about the life of J. S. B. Haldane, when experts agreed that for that very reason, i.e. the expansion of specialist knowledge, we should not see again the likes of Haldane. It would simply be impossible for one mind, however exceptional it might be, to be at the frontiers of knowledge across a wide field and translate that knowledge in a popular form. So there is a far greater stress on teachers than in previous times when advances in knowledge had not accelerated to the same extent.

Add to that the multitude of organisational change required by legislation - eg. the 1986 and 1988 Education Acts - and you have a recipe for acute overload for schools.

Because those in schools tend to be idealists, their inability to cope causes enormous guilt.

So it is as well for schools to be clear about the difference between *work* of which there is too much and which causes a feeling of guilt, panic, helplessness and inadequacy - and *responsibility* which is often badly distributed. Responsibility for something is after all having the final say about it: it is taking the lead and providing a vision of how things could be.

The job description of the 1987 Pay and Conditions Act was so unhelpful to staff development because it didn't, as so many job descriptions do not, draw a distinction between *jobs to be done* and *taking responsibility* for it.

The wisest schools ensure that the contracts for *their* teachers emphasise no more than two or three principal accountabilities - matters for which the teacher is the lead person in the school - and three or four secondary accountabilities - matters on which the teacher is a supporting person in the formulation of policy. Those are the important matters: they will give the teacher the energy to contribute to the whole life of the school and in doing so they will also offer the teacher fulfilment and satisfaction.

A Sample Job Description

Apart from taking part in the whole professional life of the school which is committed to successful teaching and learning and requires of all members of staff tutorial responsibility and the support of others in the usual administrative matters of the school, you have the following **principal** accountabilities:

- taking the lead in conjunction with departmental colleagues in establishing mathematical priorities and practices of the school

- ensuring in conjunction with departmental colleagues and the school's administration that the department is adequately staffed and resourced

- as a result of the above, establishing with colleagues and the curriculum leader of the school agreed criteria to show how progressively more children in the school may develop their mathematical talents

You have also the following **secondary** accountabilities:

- contributing appropriately through the school's curriculum review process to the overall curriculum development of the school

- taking the lead from time to time, with agreed criteria for *planning, organising* and *reviewing* one aspect of cross-curricular work

- taking part in some aspect of extra-curricular activity

- monitoring in support of Miss Julian the effectiveness of the PSE programme in the upper school.

Of course the whole issue of responsibility is best tackled at the time people are appointed. The work undertaken in preparing a background "position statement" for job applicants and the principal and secondary accountability list for the particular post is vital. Moreover it needs to be shared among all staff. I particularly admired the school which devoted a part of the school notice board entirely to that purpose so that as jobs came up, the fruits of the preparatory work were regularly displayed. Of course the deputy in charge would draw the attention of the whole staff as the occasion demanded, to the details for the new vacancy. And in that school the process of appointment meant that those involved in the newcomer's principal and secondary accountabilities would take part in some aspect of the interviewing and appointment process, even when there was only one applicant. (After all, sometimes the wise school knows when not to appoint.)

The school had a system for knowing who was responsible for what and there was an open system of appointments. It had, of course, different ideas about how it could be improved but they all recognised that it was a better system than they had encountered elsewhere. Significantly one of the improvements they were considering was the extension of it to non-teaching staff. Let me be clear. They had a *similar* system but the jobs were not displayed on the notice board. Moreover cross membership involving teaching and non-teaching staff in appointment processes is at a very tentative stage, but they argue that it is bound to improve the staff's shared sense of common purpose.

Permitting circumstances

Once teachers (and others) have their *responsibilities* made clear, they desperately need *permitting circumstances*. At its simplest this has an obvious meaning. If there are no books, materials or equipment, then the opportunity to teach well is to say the least restricted. So the link to the environment (see chapter 3) is obvious and of primary importance: it is analogous to the basic human need of food and warmth.

Three very important matters sometimes get neglected.

Teams

First there is the need to ensure that teachers can work *in teams*: that means not merely the obvious clustering of subject interest rooms so that resources are shared but also how whole year groups will be registered.

- Within departments is there the facility for team teaching if it is needed?

- How can the department or faculty head have the physical help to build teamwork?

- Are there notice boards which show the intellectual curiosity of the faculty?

- If there is emphasis on the home group or the year group, how are those activities physically fostered?

- Can dining or social areas be used to the advantage of the teaching team effort, either of the department, the year/home or the school?

The Staffroom

Secondly there is the question of the staffroom. Here I shall make enemies. You can gain a pretty strong clue to a school's success by its staffroom. If there is the issue of peer group pressure among pupils so there is amongst staff.

There used to be the bridge corner in my early years of teaching. It was great fun but it was the enemy of real thought and debate. More recently and alarmingly there has emerged the snooker table and the darts board. Some people will say I exaggerate. I do not. Quite simply the staffroom conventions, even the walls, are a barometer of a school's success. Conversations can be dominated either by backbiting or by debate about children's progress. There can be social chatter with no cutting edge or debates about interests that might inform the school's progress. Walls can be the repository for the cynical cartoon or more positively the latest 'thought provoking piece' about some educational matters. Bridge, darts and snooker - and let us be clear, I am a devotee of all three - shouldn't dominate. That is not to say that there shouldn't be some provision for that. Why not provide perhaps a separate social area available to staff, parents and pupils alike and part of committee practice? It shouldn't be in a staffroom, however.

Resource technician

The third point of neglect in teachers' physical permitting circumstances is their access to a unit staffed by non-teaching colleagues who are devoted to the production of materials to support their teaching and children's learning. It is bound up with the question of resource-based learning or flexible learning as it is now sometimes called. Teachers will find that the use of such approaches will be considerably enhanced if there is a unit properly organised and devoted to their service. So many good plans in that direction have foundered on the organisation and provision of non-teaching backup to the best intentioned of schemes. The same problem exists where large schools fail to staff adequately the library or resource centre. (See *Resources for Flexible Learning*, Book 3 of this series.)

It is important that teachers are encouraged to take risks.

There is however something far more important to teachers' permitting circumstances than the physical. Put simply, *do teachers work in surroundings in which it is permissible - even encouraged - that they should try out new ideas?* After all in unlocking any child's mind they need to keep fresh their sense of intellectual curiosity: they need to be pushing back the frontiers of their knowledge of how some children learn and how information skills and attitudes can be learned and developed more successfully. The best teachers take risks and when they do, they need to know they will be backed.

One headteacher I know put it simply by saying that she really hoped - and told teachers she hoped - that they would take risks but that when it was really risky and might get her into a fix either with parents or governors, they would tell her: not that she would stop them but that she would be prepared to back them. Amazingly she would remind them occasionally that she hadn't been taken to the limit of saying' no' for some time.

New experiences

The third aspect of staff development is the need of all staff for 'new experiences'. People need new experiences to keep them intellectually stimulated. To some extent, of course, that happens in the classroom or in departmental meetings or in whole school activities. It can be a new job: certainly to make a career in simply one set of school surroundings is less broadening than to have experience of three, four or five different settings. Teachers and others argue long and hard about 'fly-by-nights' or people 'who think only of their career' to denigrate those who hop from one position to another without ever staying long enough to prove anything. Certainly a stay of less than three, four or five years, in one set of circumstances, is unlikely to mean that you give as much as you receive. Get much beyond seven, eight or nine years however, and there is a real risk of becoming stale.

I lingered a while over writing that because I have myself spent less than three years in one place: the first occasion was my first job in teaching, where I certainly felt that the school as a whole gained less than I did from the experience. On the other hand I felt, after eleven years as Education Officer in Oxfordshire, that I was in imminent danger of not securing the best for the organisation as a result of staleness. Staleness is the real issue: it is a personal thing and will vary according to the individual and a multitude of circumstances. Of course people can gain career promotion or simply an interesting change in the same place.

> Mrs Hughes is the Head of a Primary School. When she arrived she inherited staff all of whom had been at the school in the same classroom for at least eight years. They sat in the staff room in the same chairs. All were in their mid thirties and forties. After she had talked to all of them individually she didn't have to prompt three of the staff who separately asked if they could do something more than teach the same age of children in the same room in the same way for the next twenty years! It was natural and easy, by herself teaching their classes, to get the three to start discussions on the various differences between six, eight and ten year olds respectively which happened to be their responsibility. Soon they suggested a change of teaching for a year. Before long two other members of staff were asking to have the same opportunity. Even the remaining three could be persuaded to change classrooms.

At secondary level such changes are easier to engineer either at the departmental or school level simply because the school's timetable will require some change of teaching experience from year to year. In one secondary school some of the responsibilities are swapped every three years so that new eyes can be brought to the development of the same problem. Often this is restricted to the senior management team of three or four or tive. It is perfectly possible however to design principal or secondary accountabilities which can be shared at all levels of staff management. It is necessary to be quite firm about the need for colleagues to try something new. Otherwise there is a real danger that work is something that is done almost on automatic pilot and that the only sources of stimulation and new experiences come from experience outside home.

Of course you know you are on a winner when you find members of staff who, off their own bat, ask if they can try something new out in the school, either as an extra curricular club or as a different set of teaching experiences. Moreover the teacher I met before the summer holidays, sitting on a wall in a Stoke-on-Trent high school, was a headteacher's dream. She was off to the deserts of America for her summer holidays, she said. When I enquired further, it was part pleasure but part the need she feels to have vivid experiences which will excite her teaching in the forthcoming year. In exactly the same way you will be able to spot the long suffering spouse of a primary teacher who is always collecting things on holidays.

Above all however, under the need for *new experiences*, it is essential to enter a plea for a proper set of experiences under the broad heading of Inset. Teachers, just like any other staff, need to have the stimulation of a fresh slant on old ideas and the chance to learn new skills.

Up to the mid 1980s with the introduction of Baker Days, Inset was something somebody might be experiencing as a term or a year's secondment on what was called the 'Pool' - so called because the cost of all but 25% of the teacher's salary was 'pooled' as a nationally shared cost among all authorities. Very few teachers enjoyed such secondment: in some LEAs none at all. The reason for this was of course the 25% residual cost. The LEAs reckoned, falsely, that there was thus a net cost of 25% extra since somebody had to do the job of the person seconded.

That it was false reasoning I discovered one day in a crisis as an Education Officer in Oxfordshire. The tale is worth the telling.

> My Chair of Committee was one Brigadier Roger Streatfeild, a
> wonderful man to whom I owe a great deal, not least the room to
> make mistakes, take risks and know I could rely on his good
> natured support even when I had been verging on the outrageous.
> Roger Streatfeild loved a fight and it was my job to satisfy his
> insatiable appetite for battles by providing him with the right fight.

In 1979/80 we were experiencing falling rolls and looked like having 200 too many teachers.

'Shoot them,' said the Brigadier cheerfully. I looked suitably pained and warily explained that while that was an option in war time it wasn't something you did to school teachers in the 1980s. 'Well, sack them' was the next equally unhelpful suggestion. I explained about morale - remember this was 1979/80 before such issues became more commonplace in the wake of rate and poll capping. In the end, with one or two mutterings about my provenance, especially its ILEA connections, the Brigadier was deflected.

Once I had translated the situation into talk of vital ground captured and defended by a thin red line of teachers, the Brigadier was listening again with some animation. I explained also the Pool and its facility to send people off on courses which of course I likened to intellectual assault courses.

"So what is the problem?" he asked impatiently. Cautiously I explained the 25% but then the obvious loophole - namely that if the person seconded was sufficiently senior (and the ground rules made this extremely likely by stipulating that people on secondment had to have taught for at least five years) the total cost of the replacement would be less even when one added the 25% than would be the case if the senior teacher involved remained where he or she was.

The Brigadier was interested and so eventually was the County Treasurer. Within a short time we were seconding hundreds of teachers a year for one, two or three terms - some even on different courses for two years.

Soon we learnt all the problems of such a system which was hardly surprising, given the circumstances I have described of its birth. Some of the difficulties were obvious; for instance, that good teachers would find some of the courses they attended in higher education too theoretical and irrelevant. Even when that was not the case, there was the problem of re-entry to the school. Their going had been a privilege - and in one or two cases moreover they were not seen as good teachers which of course put at risk the good name of the scheme. Given the size of the programme and the speed of its introduction mistakes of that sort were inevitable. It is not that the candidate should always be amongst the strongest: after all, in-service training has its place in extending the skills of those with potential. But they should always be amongst the most deserving.

Nevertheless even when not expressed, staff doubts included a certain amount of sniffiness about the cost and disruption to children. Colleagues were seen to be having a good time while others were bearing the heat and burden of the day. Sometimes the return of the seconded teacher was not planned: so they felt frustrated having been engaged in activity which they thought was valuable to the school only to find on their return, that nobody was interested. Worse still were the occasions when insensitive school management just let the prodigal loose on an unplanned staff in-service occasion, thus reinforcing all the worst suspicions of the rest of school colleagues. Even more occasionally and injudiciously, the wanderer returned would pipe up at a staff meeting on an issue using phrases such as 'conceptual framework' and 'theoretical paradigm' causing some wry glances and and not so concealed digs among colleagues. Indeed the most usual outcome on return from courses in such circumstances is either a gradual resocialisation of the member of staff or their departure to another job.

All those dangers can be avoided if only in-service experiences are properly *planned*, *organised* and *provided for*.

I started with the Oxfordshire experience. We soon realised our problem: indeed in fairness anticipated much of it. For example we differentiated amongst the various needs.   There was the secondment for in-service which was an individual need: this might be the need for a new skill or the extension of existing skills.   It might even be the need of someone who has been doing the same exhausting job for seven or eight years for some refreshment which would revive them spiritually. A change of job or responsibility, as has been instilled elsewhere, often achieves the same result: but it is an *individual* matter which requires careful counselling and consultation. Secondment for that purpose is indeed a privilege. I confess I have felt the need for it many times and never yet managed to arrange it.

More important by far is the *collective* agenda which can often satisfy the individual need as well. This may be within a school or even a department: it may equally be amongst a group of schools where there is a strong inter-school determination to cooperate. In the days of the Pool, Oxfordshire saw the need for this in order to avoid some of the pitfalls which I have described earlier. I remember in 1981 we established the 'skills project': it was a scheme whereby five schools were persuaded that they needed to give a greater prominence to the development of skills within the curriculum as opposed to the old heavy emphasis on information.

(Remember this was before TVEI, GCSE, Records of Achievement - so forgive its rather faded emphasis.) Each school took three full-time equivalent secondments over two years: each school had a leader and the other secondments were held by twelve different people enjoying a term each secondment. So in staffs of forty to fifty about a quarter were heavily involved in what became a joint curriculum development project. It ensured that all the five schools were brought together from time to time in order to share their different interpretations of the same set of experiences. Of course they needed no telling to find ways in the meantime in which different pairs of teachers who happened to be on secondment would find time to share out tasks and compare notes.

 The outcome was an experience which many of the teachers found enriching and certainly it helped the curriculum development of each of the schools in a profound way.

Of course the objection can be raised that the Pool is no more: that GRIST, LEATGS and GEST make the telling of such a tale not particularly useful to schools faced with different problems. Yet I would argue that the tale merely illustrated what we had very occasionally seen the successful school achieve from its own resources. Three examples come to mind:

Case Illustration One
A secondary school decided to accept a greater contact ratio (85%) in order that one member of staff could be released as a float to support a regular release of staff from a particular departmental area, in order that the department concerned could pursue its own plan to develop the curriculum. This was achieved by visits over a year to other schools, the culling and preparation of information and teaching materials and the adoption of some new approaches to learning and teaching. The same scheme rotated to different departments and has been going for seven years.

Case Illustration Two
Another primary school of four teachers had a headteacher who had half a week teaching commitment. She used one morning of the other half of her week in order to take sixty youngsters with volunteer parents on a planned dramatic production, while the two release teachers visited schools together and planned a joint curriculum change. The second half of the day (also part of her non-teaching time) the same headteacher spent in teaching one of the groups while the two teachers concerned returning from their visit taught the other class together and compared notes.

Case Illustration Three
Another secondary school's leadership actually allows a planned
day a week extra to a department for a term. The extra supply
colleague teaches in rotation classes so that joint team teaching
and/or curricula planning can happen. Yet another example has
been included in the leadership section where senior managers
have used their own teaching obligations to relieve departments for
collective curriculum development and planned observation of
other lessons.

(Robert Powell, in chapter 8 of *Resources for Flexible Learning*, illustrates
how *teams* can share, for example a 0.1 secondment.)

The collective use of inservice in this way overcomes the isolation of
teaching as an activity and enhances the shared values of the staff as well as
enabling the plans made in collective review to be translated from fond
aspirations to reality.

**It would be folly for the school not to link the individual
aspiration for further qualification with the collective need
of the school.**

It can be seen from the illustrations - and once started schools are inventive
with coming up with many more variations - that the common ingredients
are *collectivity*, *planned time* and a deliberately *planned outcome* for the
activity.

I shouldn't leave this section without some acknowledgement of the
widespread feeling among teachers either that they want to improve their
paper qualifications or that they enjoy the intellectual stimulus that such a
part time course can bring. A large number of Open University initial
degree course members have been teachers and the same university's
success with the MA bears testimony to the hunger for such courses. I am
convinced that the shrewd leadership of a school recognises this and
facilitates it.

With the increased flexibility for resources brought by Local Management
of Schools, whatever the resource allocated through LEATGS, it would be
folly for the school not to use time and money for collective development
which links the individual aspiration of the member of staff for further
qualification with the collective need of the school. The wise Polytechnic,
College or University with far sighted LEAs will make that more rather than
less likely by modularising courses.

Respect and recognition

The fourth need of staff is for respect and recognition.

Simply because teaching is a fairly isolated activity its success needs to be recognised. There is precious little respect and recognition for teachers which the following lovely poem from the TES so graphically illustrates:

> "Who'd be a teacher?" is what we've all said.
> When at something past midnight we've crawled into bed,
> And thought of the morrow with certain misgiving;
> This can't be the best way to earn me a living.
> "Who'd be a teacher?" I'm sure you've exclaimed,
> When once more in the papers the teachers are blamed
> For hooligans, drugs and graffiti, and crimes;
> It must be our fault - we've been told enough times.
> Who'd be a teacher? It just isn't rational,
> And now we must all teach the curriculum national;
> Targets are set, and each child we'll test.
> And teacher will know what to do with the rest.
> Who'd be a teacher, when some half-witted pundit
> Gets a half-witted theory, and half-wit to fund it.
> Then duly announces "Your methods are wrong;
> Children learn best if you teach them in song."
> Who'd be a teacher? We don't need more pay,
> Just look at the length of our holiday;
> And the hours aren't bad, nine until four;
> So why aren't they queuing ten deep at the door?
> Who'd be a teacher? Well, I've no regret
> That I'm leaving. I'm willing to make a small bet
> There's a smidgeon of envy in those remaining,
> Who know in the future there'll be more complaining.
> Who'd be a teacher; we all know the score;
> Trials and frustrations we've all had, and much more.
> But we've all felt the glow when a child has succeeded,
> And the pride that we've helped to give what that child needed.
> Who'd be a teacher? I'll make a confession,
> I'm proud that I've been in this great profession.
> And on this occasion I'll raise my glass -
> "To Teachers - God bless them - they're top of the class!"

(Jennie Radley, former Headteacher of Simms Cross County Infants School, Widnes. The poem is reproduced with kind permission of the TES.)

So how can all staff be *respected* and *recognised*? Clearly most of it has to come from within the school. First there is the planned visit by the headteacher to classrooms and departments: there is the seeking out of matters to praise, both by a handwritten note of thanks and the spoken word. At staff meetings the wise leader will always seek to find ways of thanking colleagues by name for particular contributions. There is also the governors' meeting. There is the need for example to ensure that the Chair of Governors seeks to praise the staff as well as the headteacher when there are public occasions.

It would be easy to elaborate to all the techniques of good management of interpersonal relationships. It is after all the one quality required above all others as we implied in the section on Leadership. It is certainly the key to staff development.

Set aside a time each day for thanking people.

People's personal needs require the most sensitive thought backed by a good system to make sure the thought is translated into action. You simply cannot leave to chance that you will regularly remember to have a word with a person and to thank them. One of the best leaders I know used to set aside a quarter of an hour each day specifically for the purpose of writing notes to people about things he had observed that were good or that people had told him were.   Once the climate of positive reinforcement is established, it is that much easier to pick up on the occasional point of criticism which is of course always best done in private. Every now and then we will need that jolt too.

Respect and recognition however in successful schools are not merely a 'top-down' process. It is particularly important among peer groups. So teachers can make their own life more enjoyable simply by resolving to do things for each other. There is a social cement in staff rooms which is as intangible as it is real: it comes from shared social occasions.

> The teacher told me of the old days when they had gathered in each other's houses in the evenings, each bringing a dish or some drink and how they had stayed up to eleven, midnight or sometimes one in the morning, working on some scheme or other. You cannot legislate for that but you can create a climate even in the wake of the pernicious 1265 hours where it is more rather than less likely, where teachers will simply want to give much more time together.

After all the outcome is a much pleasanter working atmosphere. In all this talk of staff development, it will be noted that so far I have not mentioned staff appraisal. That is simply because I have not yet met a successful school which over a sustained period has a staff appraisal scheme which would reckon it had been instrumental in affecting positively their success. Nor significantly is it highlighted as important in the research in America where studies on effective schooling have a long history and there is much experience of appraisal.

Before the period of teachers' strikes and other action intended to disrupt the normal working of the school (1985/86) the issue of staff appraisal was not discussed. A few pioneering schools had what they called either staff development schemes or self evaluation schemes for individuals. Most of those went into suspension during the period of teachers' disruption: very few revived. The next great tranche of appraisal comes as a result of a 'top-down' government inspired interest in the subject which has been confused variously with merit pay, *weeding out bad teachers* and target setting.

Charles Handy reported Skinner as saying that "the biggest problem with American industry and commerce is staff appraisal..........people take six months preparing for it and six months recovering from it."

Notwithstanding these cautionary, even negative observations, I know that many headteachers now swear by staff appraisal on early evidence of its possibilities and that in any case it is now only a matter of time before it is a commonplace feature of school life. I have illustrated opposite a flow diagram which serves as a model of how to introduce staff appraisal: in a sense it serves equally well as an example of how to go about introducing *any* change.

The key feature is to match the teacher's vision with the vision of the school as a whole.

Probably the key common factor which successful staff appraisal schemes include is the need for a systematic method through which every member of staff has the opportunity to discuss progress with the person to whom they are responsible. Without calling it staff appraisal of course, successful leaders have always ensured that, at not too distant intervals, they have a purposeful discussion with each member of staff or ensure that some senior colleague does.

A model flowchart for introducing appraisal

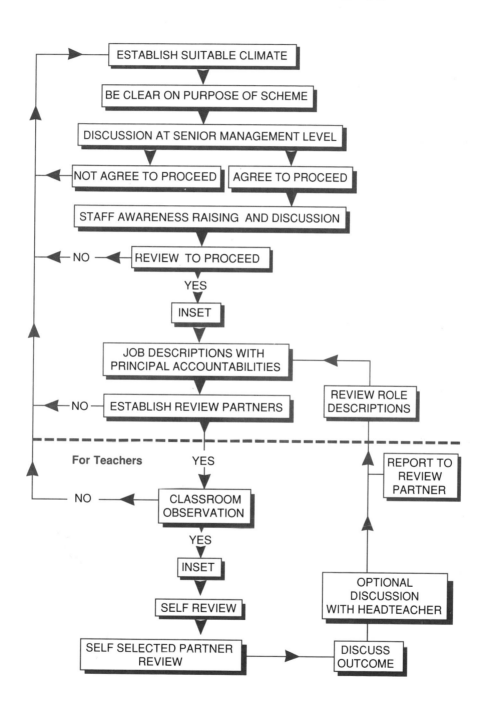

The agendas for such discussions include for the teacher:

- a vision for what his/her job could become

- the way in which the leader might better accommodate that vision

- many questions about the parts of the job the teacher enjoys best

- a discussion of the teacher's principal and secondary accountabilities and when (rather than whether) there might be interest in them being changed in some respect

- personal career aspirations

- some agreed further date when discussions might resume either with the leader or the leader's colleague.

Throughout these discussions it is important to keep finding ways in which the leader of the discussion can find a fit between the teacher's vision and the vision of the school as a whole. All that seems to be easily achievable: if that is what is meant by staff appraisal schemes, that is fine - indeed a positive safeguard against paving the road with good intentions.

Many staff appraisal schemes however incorporate within them teacher observation: and teacher observation is too important to run the risk of being linked with an activity which could be seen as negative.

One of the scandals of our schools is the way in which we have continued to allow teaching to be such an isolated and private activity.

After all in most other walks of life, particularly the practice of a skill, we reckon to learn considerably when we are aided by a check list of criteria in observing others doing the same thing. Consider sport or the arts and the way in which the experts exhaustively analyse the techniques of the various performers. Indeed in teacher training it is also so. Yet after teacher training and certainly after the Induction Year it is very rare for the teacher to have the opportunity to observe another teach or to be observed.

In that process, the observing is rather more important than being observed even though it is often the latter that is emphasised. After all, when you observe another doing the same or a similar job, you bring to the task of observing your own set of favourite techniques. If it is an open-minded observation you will often see the most subtle and sometimes the most striking alternative possibilities which can be tried out in your own style when you return to your daily task. You make your own private judgements about the match of the practice you observe with your own, reassuring yourself about things you do better and see little things that could extend your range of skills as a practitioner. Being observed on the other hand often induces a sense of defensiveness and predisposition to self-justification or deflection of criticism. We plead in mitigation a set of exceptional circumstances and certainly can easily become involved in a huge time and energy trap. That is why the model of external inspection by HMI and local Inspectors is so fraught with difficulty and has such limited potential. Of course there are exceptions to this proposition: there are among us all a few hardy individuals who find the whole process stimulating: indeed it can be, if it is not too public and the ground rules are agreed beforehand.

> I came across a school not long ago which had instituted what seemed to be an excellent scheme. The school as a whole had agreed that it should be the right of everyone of the staff to be observed and to observe another by mutual agreement and in private. So the school planned the timetable in order that each member of staff did just that for one day at least once a year. The outcome of each observation was shared privately between participants and the aim was to produce a document to be put in the Staff Handbook for future new members of staff, about what the highest common factor of agreement could be about what constitutes good teaching and learning in the particular school in question. Their plan was to modify the document from time to time.

(The issue of mutual observation is also raised in Books 2, 3 and 4 of this series.)

When I originally planned this section of the book it was to be simply staff development, and I knew I had to be careful to make the point early on about our Freudian tendency to ignore as real staff members of the community those who are not teachers. As I wrote however I knew that the section would have an emphasis on teaching and that in any case the sole justification for the development of the best in all members of staff in a school but particularly teachers is simply to enable youngsters to learn more successfully.

What is Successful Teaching and Learning?

Successful teaching is an issue as seriously and as often debated and shared in school staff rooms as what makes a school successful. Yet the two are natural, indeed inseparable bedfellows and the goal of all heads of schools should be to have the very best teaching and learning in their schools. If one of the goals of the school development plan is to find out more about successful teaching and learning and if one of the features of staff development is to arrange the time to support that activity, the school will need to start somewhere. What follow are some images of successful teaching and learning as they have been picked up by various groups of teachers in different schools.

One of the most important principles of successful teaching is surely that teachers should be *inclusive* rather than exclusive in their activity: as learners we all remember what we thought of teachers who seemed to *ignore us* settling for working with a few - or worse still even the majority - of the students who seemed able to share the mysteries of the subject or skill we were trying to learn. It is possible to observe techniques in classroom craft that are intended to be inclusive rather than exclusive: for example, the use of praise; the extent to which all members of the staff ask questions; even the position adopted by the teacher; and the arrangements for youngsters' seats, tables or desks. (This issue is explored in some depth in Book 4 of this series, *Tutoring*.)

Through the generations, various people have described what it means to be a good teacher. To create the mood I believe it difficult to better a quotation from Thring, the Victorian headteacher, to whose views I was first introduced by Peter Newsam:

> "And there I learnt the secret of St Augustine's golden key, which though it be of gold it is useless unless it fits the wards of the lock. And I found the wards I had to fit - the minds of those little street boys, very queer and tortuous affairs and I had to set about cutting and chipping myself in every way to try and make myself into the wooden key, which should have the one merit of a key, however common it might look, the merit of fitting the lock and unlocking the mind and opening the shut chambers of the heart."

There can be few teachers who do not recognise what Thring was talking about: interestingly he went on to describe the need for teacher training in the following letter to the Times in 1886:

> "But no one can unlock a door without a key. The world is full of locked doors. Every child is a locked door but where are the keys? Where is there any distinct conviction that any key is wanted? That such an article as a key to mind exists? The sloppy idea of education which prevails, reduced to shape and practice, needs a

set of trucks all in a row, memory trucks with navvies pitching ballast into them against time. Or not doing so as the case may be. But loading up other people's facts is not training minds. One more point demands notice. There are not only no keys but the present system prevents keys being made. A key is adapted to fit intricacies into winding in and out of queer passages. The successful scholar however is a man who has run through his work smoothly and found the least obstacles. And these are the men who are selected to deal with the greatest number of obstacles."

If one discounts the inevitable male imagery of the period there is much in the point that the most successful teachers are often those with first hand experience of the difficulty of learning.

Earlier in this section I argued for the right of a teacher to observe another at least once a year. It would be a fairly pointless exercise unless the two participants had prepared beforehand a set of issues which were to be observed. Moreover the start of the observation needs to be from the moment the teacher starts school until the moment they leave at the end of the school day. After all most of time in teaching is in preparation, marking and follow-up.

I followed the three teachers on three separate days in their schools. This is an unusual but instructive activity. Many have followed children - pupil pursuit it's called - few have followed the teacher. Time and space do not permit full descriptions.

Joan is in her late twenties, fair haired and energetic: she teaches as others breathe. Her day starts at 7.50 a.m. at school in the north west with a check on a future experiment; it closes at 6.15 p.m. after a staff meeting. Besides her lessons she does 'break duty' and takes two lunch hour clubs. In the 'inbetween' times she finds time for 100 conversations with separate youngsters who are attracted to her like rivets to a magnet.

Roger is in his mid thirties, is corduroyed and bearded; solidly built Roger starts at 8.30 a.m. and had a parent evening so I left him at 6.30 p.m. for a snack. In his full timetabled day he managed 400 individual conversations in lessons with youngsters: he never raised his voice; the overwhelming majority of exchanges were positive and full of praise, a small percentage were neutral or gave information. There were no rebukes. All his youngsters entered the room and worked with a verve and without needing to be told.

Anne in her late thirties wears flowered dresses and has capacious arms. Quiet, a smile is never far from her lips and never leaves her eyes. Her class of seven year olds, thirty strong, would do anything for her - especially learn and develop their talents. Her day starts at 8.15 a.m. She has two adults, one an unpaid parent, the other a salaried ancillary who are the orchestra to her skilful leadership. Her children enjoy much positive adult conversation - all punctuated by the question 'why' and all supported by gentle promise. There is the low purposeful hum of busy conversation - the hallmark of a successful primary classroom. Anne takes no break at all until 3.30 p.m. The subsequent staffroom coffee break is full of conversation about children and new techniques of children's learning.

All three filled their lunch hour with activity for their young friends: for Roger an electronics club, for Joan netball practice and some extra sixth form enrichment and for Anne a recorder group.

What had these excellent teachers in common? In a text book fashion one could describe the general skills as threefold.

Firstly they were all *diagnosticians* - diagnosticians in the sense of having met, remembered and observed the hundreds, if not thousands of youngsters ever learning more about the mystery of the young mind by cross coding to previous cases. Indeed Joan said "I remember James who was a real friend of mine - don't you remember him? He left last year to go to university .....he had just your problem, Anne. I think I know how we can overcome it". Of course it is not just experience, it is also the linking of the theory of their trade to that experience that makes them good diagnosticians. Like all theories and knowledge, those affecting education have moved on. We do know more through research and speculation than we did twenty years ago. All these teachers are ceaselessly pursuing their own learning: their talk is full of articles read recently or spoken about or courses attended. The diagnosis comes both from long practice and sharply honed theory.

Secondly they are *facilitators*. They know what is the next best step for youngsters' learning. Roger walked across a classroom with an open book clawed from some display shelf. "Hey what do you think of this?" to one of his class "Doesn't it fit your problem?" In the next breath, he asked another lad to go and look at some equipment being used in an experiment taking place in a nearby laboratory. On another occasion a sixth former asked to take down and borrow a display poster as research for his further weekend project.

Thirdly they are all *animateurs*, a strange French word the meaning of which is difficult to capture in English. Was it the *shared warm touch* with hand and eye so clear in Anne's work with the primary youngsters? Was it the *warm interest* in the eyes of all three teachers: none of them had even a touch of the glazed preoccupied mid-distance in their eyes? Was it the *shared glee of discovery* in Joan's electronic circuitry lesson? Was it the *enthusiasm*? I am sure they all really like all their youngsters, even the unlikeliest, even the ones who were unkempt and dirty. Was it in Roger's way of picking up and re-establishing the *esteem* of the young man who had required an earlier rebuke? So those are the general qualities - diagnosis, facilitation, enthusiastic confidant/animateur - I just cannot get the last quality into words. But there is so much more in the observation of them as they ply their trade. I want to pick out eight features.

1) Display and Welcoming.

The good teacher, in the primary school especially, knows the value of visual surroundings of the youngsters. "Surround them" said Edward Thring, "with things that are noble". Well yes, but let them see their own things, let them also see work of excellence, let the room be colourful, let some of the display reinforce language policy and high standards. Let's banish the ubiquitous drawing pin and banish the unremoved scraps of Blu Tack. Replace them by corners with a graph showing continuing research in Anne's classroom. And what of the mathematical puzzle? What of the verity of a piece of eternal inspiration from an ancient or modern poet? And is the eye level right for the child and how often does it change? And does it pervade the whole school? Does work show sharp observation and imagination? All three teachers knew the answers.

2) Good Preparation and Changing Style.

All three teachers in their different ways had prepared their work. Each consulted a large looseleaf folder before work began. There was no frantic search for forgotten implements or materials - I shall not forget Roger's laying out of strips of Sellotape in readiness for the group's next activity. In all the lessons, children worked with pace and life: groups were working at different speeds but each member of the group had an agreed task which occupied their time fully. Each teacher changed style in a number of subtle ways. There were periods of group work - sometimes there was slight competition between groups: there were periods of the class as a whole coming together and there was time for individual tasks.

Each teacher too changed pace to suit the needs of the group or the individual. Of course the research on effective classroom management whether from Leicester or Lancaster supports the effectiveness of these techniques that I observed on these three days with three excellent teachers.

Without that skill of noticing change in children teachers are not teaching.

3) Sharp Observation
Perhaps the observation of the number of exchanges with individual children - over a hundred at break and lunch time for Joan and four hundred for Roger in his lessons - is some testimony to the teacher's skill at noticing children. What I did observe in both these cases was how well they shared their interests among the different members of each class: in a way that was easier to do in the case of Anne where she was with the same children for the whole of the day. (As an aside, how much more difficult does the organisation of some large schools make the task of the good teacher: for if you teach three hundred plus children a week - by no means uncommon for the secondary school teacher - how much more taxing and superficial must be your observation of changes in children - especially if so many of such children change with each school year). To return to Anne, there is no doubt that she spent her time fairly: most received seven to nine minutes' individual attention and discussion, one received two and another fifteen minutes. Anne talked at length and with perception at the end of the day about each and every one of her pupils.

4) Good Use of Time
All teachers shared the capacity to carry out tasks simultaneously. For example children engaged in tasks to help class room management were being asked questions or otherwise receiving attention. At a trivial level the fish were fed en route to the start of a group demonstration in one of Roger's Science lessons. Moreover he was subtly effecting a silent scientific revolution by the tutorial health education programme he had arranged for the school. That was using time twice on a large scale! Each was aware of the different needs of time for different tasks in the rhythms of the day. Anne, the primary teacher, confessed to the luxury of the primary day and week. "I am in control of time rather than it of me". Even her lesson plans were more flexible: the structure, as it were, was less procrustean. All were inhibited

by the pattern of the school day, term, year which is such a dampener to the pace of a child's learning. In another place, on another occasion, one could elaborate on that but the impact of the secondary school timetable and long summer holidays and starting the school year in September rather than Easter is enormous and toxic to basic skill acquisition at both primary and secondary level. What a pity all those HMI and Ministerial documents ignore the issue totally.

5) Open Questioning - the "Why" of Education

Whether in the questions and quizzes on display on the walls, or in the open as opposed to closed style of questioning, all three teachers encouraged children to wonder why. Traditionally we are strong on the "what" (information) of education: latterly we have concentrated on the "how" (skills). Except in the case of outstanding thinking teachers, such as the ones I saw, we are less challenging about the "why" (ideas/concept) of what we do. Occasionally these three teachers simply confessed to not knowing - not only some information - but also the reasons for certain phenomena. On no such occasion however was the quest closed down: rather was the hunt stimulated.

6) Marking of Work

One teacher was having an interesting dialogue through long written exchanges at the end of essays: another was encouraging self and mutual marking on repetitive and simple tasks. All deployed positive systems. In the case of all three teachers the absence of a mark on one piece of work prompted an apology from the teacher: the work had not been overlooked, it simply required more time from the teacher to do it justice. Of course where the work was to be celebrated communally by display, no marking occurred: the act of celebration was enough. In another case a group displayed their wares in the form of a play for their peers'

7) The Hidden Curriculum

Marking, of course, is part of the hidden curriculum. It was interesting that none of the three deployed the insidious A to E norm references and value-laden systems that prevail so widely. The hidden curriculum was also in the tone of voice, in the eyes and in the bearing of the teacher. In every case all were concerned, teacher and taught alike, with the careful building of mutual confidence and real achievement. The teachers did it by the encouraging nature of their remarks: the youngsters did it by their respect of tacit and implicit codes of behaviour.

Perhaps Roger in the rather formal boys' school will stick with me most. It was the quiet way, unbeknown to the rest of the class, that he detached a youngster from a group and put him into another group with a firm but whispered rebuke en route: within minutes the boy was re-established in his own eyes and that of the teacher as he answered a class question correctly.

It was interesting too how in a formal school, where surnames were required, Roger raised the youngsters to a level of equality by calling them "Mr". In a curious way there was more equality than in a school where there is one way traffic only in Christian names. Part of the hidden curriculum is at home where literally half the children's curriculum happens. All three teachers in their conversations, their actions, their strategies talked of home background, work to be done, of contracts to be shared.

8) Energy

All three teachers were very energetic. Accustomed to often fifteen hour working days, I was nevertheless exhausted. I am increasingly under the impression that teaching is becoming a young person's profession. Joan's working day at school started before 8 a.m. and did not end until 7 p.m. Roger had a parents' evening after starting half an hour later. Anne's day was marginally shorter but even more intense.

Which other profession knows that it must work for such long hours with such a small group intensively, the more perceptive of them aware that the inflection of their voice, the manner of their bearing, the movement of their eyebrow will be having an effect on those for whom they work? All of course have preparation and marking after that, and all referred to work "in the school holidays". If not a young person's profession you need more than the average energy and a certainty of belief in the task in hand that is the pedagogic equivalent of a Hippocratic oath. *So these are the three good teachers.*

A teacher training institution - a place where of course you'd expect people to have thought about successful teaching and learning - expressed their principles about teaching are as follows:

> We believe that there are different teaching styles but that those which are successful in unlocking children's talents are informed by certain common principles and attitudes. We have found it difficult to be precise or exhaustive about the common features but their flavour is perhaps best captured by saying that those involved in this initiative want to help to produce teachers who are prepared to:

- provide equal opportunities for pupils or students to help them to become confident, competent and contributing citizens

- treat children as individuals;

- realise the powerful influence inevitably exerted by their own various models

- become supportive team members who will contribute to creating and maintaining a successful school

- present high expectations to pupils and emphasise their positive achievements

- take seriously their own professional development and remain intellectually curious

- have a healthy sense of humour and of perspective

- contribute to the greater knowledge of the profession during their career.

These are just some beginning thoughts on the real outcome of an effective school staff development policy and practice - the greater understanding by a whole school staff of what makes successful teaching and learning.

Interlude...

The In-service Day

School one

The school was cold and we huddled in overcoats on a bleak January morning.

The Head introduced the day with the encouraging "Now we all know there is nowhere where you would rather not be today than here". And a few pale smiles came from the lecture theatre with its broken seats and inadequate lighting.

He glanced at his deputy: "We were to have devoted today to special needs, weren't we Mrs Brown", but she shook her head violently and said "Pastoral care, headmaster".

"Well, yes, the same thing really," the head ploughed on and explained how they had been let down by a county advisory teacher and I had been prepared to come at short notice. At least in that if not recollecting my name he was accurate. He said I would talk about successful schools. He supposed they would learn something from people who were in ivory towers and invited his colleagues to welcome me. Personally I rather doubted his confidence.

Afterwards, in complimenting my efforts in a rather backhanded way, he ruminated on what a waste of time Baker Days usually were: they had, of course, been all right at first, after the teachers' action in bringing the staff together - "but you soon run out of ideas". Now he made most of them available to departments and for report writing. No.... he had not compared notes with other schools and supposed it would be quite useful if only there was time. He presented me with a school tie as a memento of an unforgettable occasion.

School two

As I approached the east coast town, I scrabbled on my passenger seat for the directions to the high school where I was to talk later that morning, a day for in-service training.

I regarded the AA sign casually and my eyes widened in disbelief. But there they were - all leading me to the five coastal schools' staff training day. "Next thing," I thought to myself, "there will be a welcoming banner". And there was, two hundred feet across the 1903 facade of what had once been the town's grammar school. Five coastal high schools had decided that their combined efforts for at least one day a year would bring considerable shared experience of enthusiasm and skills: they seemed to have planned it well. Moreover they made a good start.

They had gathered from 7.45 am for breakfast and settled for an hour in a darkened hall for a *Theatre in Education* professional production on school life. They then went their various ways to workshops on thirty-five different themes, ranging from cross-curricular topics through subject, pastoral, even school organisational matters - each with marching orders to produce an abstract to be printed and circulated to add to the growing 'staff development library' which the schools collectively were creating.

I have never felt more worried that I might let somebody down when I tried to throw a few ideas about to the assembled three hundred and fifty teachers on their chosen topic of 'What makes successful teaching and learning'. I marvelled that within five minutes of the end of the morning all were enjoying a buffet lunch with a glass of wine and beautifully prepared food, all served by youngsters. Afterwards at least a hundred and fifty participants repaired to the adjoining leisure centre and schools sports facility for social and recreational pursuits.

5

Organising and Maintaining Success

Making Sure the Organisation and Maintenance of Provision Diminishes Staff Stress

ANISING AND MAINTAINING SUCCESS

"I take my stand on detail." The Victorian headteacher beloved by Clegg, handed on by Peter Newsam, seems to have had a phrase for everything to do with successful schooling.

Get the 'bits and pieces' right.

It is worth concluding this brief glimpse into what makes a good school by returning to the cycle of management outlined at the beginning.

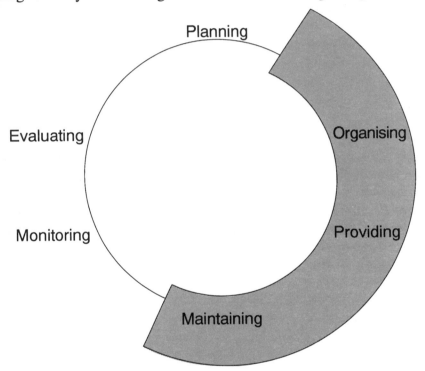

What has gone before has dwelt on *planning*, on the need to secure an overall sense of direction and purpose; of the need for vision and being able to see the wood for the trees. After all, the leadership function discharged properly should secure all of that. Moreover the chapter on collective review has emphasised the essential connection between good teaching - indeed good schooling - and the need to monitor and evaluate.

I used to be puzzled by schools saying "We are simply so busy keeping the system going, dealing with daily crises, that we have got no time to think. It is good to have people like you coming in from time to time to raise us above the level of the daily grind". Of course, schools which say that are often modest: very frequently they are the very schools which show that sense of healthy self criticism rather than self justification which is one of the hallmarks of a good school. Nevertheless they are saying that once a term starts, there is precious little time, even in the best run school, to do other than to spend one's time keeping the ship afloat; mostly it is a question of slight adjustments but often quite a bit of putting fingers in the dyke. There is, for example, the ever present daily reality of members of staff being off ill unexpectedly and therefore how to deal with the unpopular issue of 'cover'.

How well the school is organised and maintained - the administration of the school - vitally affects the lives of teachers.   If there are constant fouls-up in the administration it is almost impossible to avoid staff stress and loss of morale accumulating during the school year: moreover it saps the highest common factor of *shared values* and *common purpose* which should be that of the good school.

A teacher remarked to me the other day that with the best will in the world it is almost impossible not to be put out when somebody tells you at 3 pm that at 5 pm you are meant to be presenting a paper on your curriculum area to the school governors. This was the first you had heard about the request, although later you discover at the meeting they had made the request four months previously! In another school it was seen in the snatched staffroom exchange one afternoon, about the parental consultation that same evening. It transpired nobody had thought fit to send out the invitations. The mind boggles at the fury which would have happened if all the staff had turned up to an empty hall!   Stories like that are legion and while in retrospect the farce involved can be guaranteed to bring laughter to staff room stories, at the time there is precious little humour.

Are there, therefore, simple rules which good schools observe in order not to induce too many fouls-up?

Staff handbooks are so much wasted paper........they are misplaced and rarely read.

The first feature I have noticed is a *good administrative handbook* in loose leaf form, perhaps in those plastic covered envelopes within a ring binder - kept in the school office, in the staff room and within all departments. Sometimes it is incorporated in the staff handbook although in practice if that is all there is, the handbook is rarely used. Rather it is the case that the 'admin book' is in the form it is because it will be referred to frequently and the arrangements will change on an annual/termly basis but never in between because there is a chaos of communication otherwise. The book is a standing item on the agenda of staff meetings once a term, so that replacement sheets can be inserted and rehearsed and the smooth running kept under review.

The book quite simply is an exhaustive list of organisational arrangements with one sheet for each such arrangement. At the top of each sheet is the name of the person responsible for ensuring that the work is carried out and below is a brief description of the rationale for the activity followed by a list of dates and the work that has to be carried out by all members of the community in order that the task can be successfully completed.

The larger the school (with all the overlong and stretched lines for personalised communication which is inevitable in a large organisation), the more crucial the book of administration is. In smaller schools they are important but can be simpler and rely more on word of mouth, custom and practice. Sadly so many large schools make the mistake of pinning everything down in this way so that the book of administration can be the '*expletive deleted blankety blank blank book*' which rules the lives of everyone and stifles any initiative. The trick for large schools, like large organisations of any sort, is to judge what has to be determined at school level and what can be left to the department, the house, the year group or whatever. In some circumstances it may be sufficient for the smaller unit - the department we'll say - simply to follow certain common principles and, with a book of administration for themselves, to supplement the simpler school book.

There is little doubt that schools much beyond 1000 pupils in size have to think very seriously about such issues and come to their own judgement about what is best for them.

However it is organised, I cannot imagine that a school can run as well as it should if there aren't either at the school level or the departmental level simple descriptive sheets covering:

Parental involvement

- Parents' evenings

- Records of achievement and reports

- Parent involvement as joint educators, eg. paired/shared reading

- Parental letters and visits to and from parents

Governors

- Arrangements for meetings, agenda setting, agenda compilation and despatch, minute writing and circulation

- Governors' involvement in school events and activity

Pupil Welfare

- Class tutor relationship to year/house

- Attendance registers and arrangements for absence

- Report writing

- Praise, merit and sanction system

- Special needs

Staff Welfare

- Appointments - arrangements for..... including briefing details, advertisements, interviews, letters and industrial practice

- Staff common room arrangements - teaching and non-teaching

- Learning resources, material support, e.g. library/resources, IT back-up, etc.

- Inset opportunities - teaching and non-teaching arrangements for the five staff development days, etc.

- (Staff appraisal scheme)

Data

- Pupil Information

- Staff Information

- Whole School Information

- Finances

Curriculum and Assessment

- Definitions of different forms of talent

- Whole school assessment procedures

- Individual and pupil assessments

- Cross-curricular planning and delivery

- Departmental/Subject matters

Events

- Parents

- Performances

- Trips

- PTA

- Meetings for staff

- Meetings for governors

- Awards

- Sports

- Examinations/Tests/SATS

Non-Teaching Staff

One of the key features in a successful school is how the weight of the school's running and organisation are shared with non-teaching staff. A good example of this is the key role of the school's secretary or administrator. The illustration opposite shows the crucial role such a person plays in the organisation of the school.

Whatever the size of the school this position has within it the potential to affect for good or ill the school's progress. The person is the recipient of intended and unintended confidences, he/she has to judge what and how vital messages are conveyed, how a crisis can be defused or, if they get it wrong, wilfully or otherwise, a minor incident can be transformed into a time and energy consuming crisis. Governors, staff, parents and pupils will have a habit of seeing the secretary/administrator as the person they can trust and with whom they can relax.

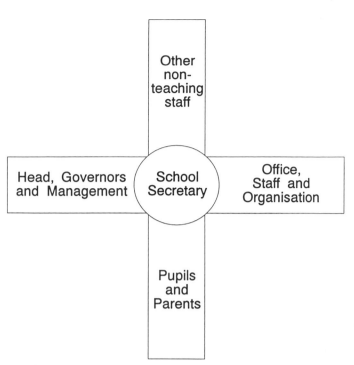

The school secretary or Administrator

In the examples of school administration which follow it is significant that the school in question frequently pairs teaching with non-teaching staff. The intention of providing these examples is not simply to show good practice in the particular activity involved, though they may be interesting to all schools since the same issues have to be tackled by them, but rather to illustrate the theme of taking care of the *bits and pieces.*

Certainly it needs to be someone's expressed role to look after the well-being of all the non-teaching staff. It will very frequently be a non-teacher who is the first person encountered whether on the telephone or in a visit.

Queen Elizabeth School Administration Handbook

Homework

Person(s) responsible - **John Wainwright** (English Dept), **Ann James** (School Admin. Assist.)

The school's policy for homework is attached as an annex to this sheet: it is also included in the school brochure and staff handbook. The next regular date for collective review is **June 1992**. **John Wainwright** is responsible for policy interpretation and will trawl views on the possible ways of improving our policies and practices prior to the review. The normal rules of collective review will of course apply.

Practice

The responsibility for the setting and marking of homework is shared by all staff according to a timetable diary for homework produced by **Joan Collins** at the same time as the normal school timetable in the July of one year for implementation the following September. **Ann James** is responsible for ensuring that all staff are reminded of that as part of their general teaching information pattern in the second half of August.

- Homework in the two weeks before school exams is revision and the revision policy document applies.

- In the other four weeks devoted to intensive activity - school performances, events, visits - during which timetables are suspended, it will be noted that special homework practices will apply. (See Policy)

- Homework should be a natural extension of school work or in the case of Year 7, 9, 10 and 11, linked to each pupil's supported self-study project.

- Homework facilities exist for pupils who prefer to carry it out at school on Mondays to Thursdays inclusive in the Learning Centre, from the end of school until 5 pm. Responsibility for ensuring that pupils in Year 11 are available as 'responsible adults' for each session, is one of the duties of **Don Rogers** (Head of Year 11).

Homework - a statement of policy for parents

What do we do about homework

Teachers set tasks or activities regularly which need to be done partly or completely out of school time.   The success of the lessons and the progress of students depends on this.

The tasks take different lengths of time to complete: some take less than an hour, some go on in stages for a number of weeks. In each week of term, students normally either have some homework set or work that they can carry on with, for every subject they take. These activities arise naturally out of the work in the classroom. They are not always set on the same day each week.

Tasks have *deadlines* which are made clear to students.

Teachers check who has met the deadline and make a note of any who do not. If a student often fails to do homework without good reason, parents are informed.

Not all homework needs to be assessed. If it does, and is given in on time, it is marked promptly and returned to students for filing or storing.

As well as doing tasks set for homework, students are expected to develop their knowledge and skills independently. Teachers give advice about this.

Every student is given a *notebook* for noting down homework tasks and deadlines and ticking them off when done. Tutors check these books from time to time.

Students are welcome to stay on at school after lessons finish on Monday to Thursday to do their homework, with help if they need it. Please contact Mrs James for details, or ask the Day Tutor to do this for you.

What you can do to help

Appreciate the need for independent study and provide a place for it, as free from distractions as possible.

Support students by showing an interest and giving encouragement; ask them to explain the work to you. This can develop their understanding and their reasoning skills.

Help students to plan their time and to organise themselves so that they remember to *bring to school* each day the materials that they need, and to *take home* the work they need to do each evening. It would also help if you could sign their homework diary to show that you are doing this.

Keep in contact with us. Always feel free to come and see us. Ring if there is anything you need to know, or if you would like to make an appointment.

School Rules displayed in every classroom and the staffroom are another feature of a society which takes itself seriously. So often however the rules are created negatively. The example included below is one school's attempt to frame them positively. Admittedly it didn't have the problem posed by uniform - so often the cause of dispute:

The Abbey School

This Code of Conduct has been produced after full consultation with students, staff, parents and governors.

Introduction
Students at Abbey have the right to an education which offers them the best opportunity to attain their potential.

Teachers are here to create the circumstances for this to happen, support staff, governors, parents and officers of the LEA to assist in the process.

It is the right of every individual at Abbey to do these things without being hindered by others.

Guiding principles
In order that the foregoing should happen, it is essential that every one of us is:

considerate	respecting everyone else as an individual; making sure our words and actions do not cause inconvenience to anybody
courteous	being polite and helpful at all times
cooperative	being willing to work together

friendly	being on good terms with each other
hard working	doing our best
honest	being truthful
trusting	accepting that others genuinely want to help
responsible	being reliable and responsible for our actions; behaving as part of a community.

The principles in action

What this means in practice is that we should all do the following:

be punctual	avoid late arrival
speak considerately	avoid shouting, swearing and offensive language
be ready for lessons	have the necessary materials
clear up	after lessons, break and lunch;
move in an orderly way	avoid running and use paths; hold doors open for other people;
respect the environment	the grass, trees, hedges, buildings and furniture.

In lessons

It is the responsibility of teachers to:

- prepare appropriate work for all students in the group
- provide opportunities for students to be actively involved in their learning
- recognise and encourage achievement and success
- assess students' work regularly
- maintain an orderly atmosphere in the classroom.

It is the responsibility of students to:

- get on with their work to the best of their ability

- be prepared to work with anyone else in the group

- ask for help when necessary

- be prepared to wait for their turn

- accept advice and guidance from the teacher

- carry out requests from the teacher.

The bottom line

The law of the land applies at Abbey just as it does everywhere else. So, there are some things which are forbidden, not just because we may disapprove of them, but because they are against the law. These are:

- truancy
- drinking alcohol under age
- physical violence
- damage to property

- threatening behaviour
- leaving litter
- sexist behaviour and smoking by students

Every successful school will have patiently examined every aspect of its administrative arrangements to diminish the chances of it letting down the higher purposes of the school's ambitions and all the efforts of the teachers.

Colour coding saves staff stress

As far as administrative matters are concerned there's bound to be a great deal of paper. The wise school is careful about colour coding and clear bold referencing : it makes the stress of handling information overload that much easier. Consider opposite, the contents page of another school's administration book.

King Alfred's School Administration Book

Contents

Staff Organisation - Blue Section

Absence

(i)   Illness

(ii) Visits, INSET

(iii) Leaving thecampus

(iv) Setting work for supply teachers

(v)   Co-ordinator's role during absence

Addresses

Arrival in School

Charging for School Activities

Contact with outside Agencies

Curriculum

Duties

Information Technology

Internship Scheme

Lunchtime Meals and Supervision

Meetings and Communication

Oxford Certificate of Educational Achievement (O.C.E.A.)

Reviews

Secretarial/Resource Support

Use of Minibus

Visitors

Visits with Students

Social Organisation - Green Section

Assemblies - - and

Campus Use

Code of Conduct

Fire Notices

Fire Drill Positions - Fig.1

Homework - Policy for Parents

Punishments

Racism - Staff Policy

Registers

Rewards

School Aims

School Council

Times of the School Day

Planning Summaries - Yellow Section

Activities Week	Curriculum and Timetable Development
Admission of New Students During the School Year	External Examinations
Applications for INSET Courses	Higher Education Applications
Careers Guidance and Work Experience Yr 10 - Yr 11	Prospective Students and their Parents
Course Planning in Yr 9	Secondment Applications 1991-92

Appendix - Poppy Section

Staff List Caretaking	Staff List Teaching : Tutorial
Staff List Creche	Staff List Teaching : Curriculum Areas
Staff List Continuing Education	Staff List Management Team Roles
Staff List Kitchen	Role of Special Needs Support Assistants
Staff List Sports And Arts Centre	Role of Teacher in Relation to Special Needs Support Assistants
Staff List Support Staff	
Staff List Teaching : alphabetical , with timetable initials, scale points and brief role descriptions	

Appendix - White Section

Planning Calendar 1991-92	Membership of frequent meetings; list of working parties and other committees.
Holiday Dates	

Interlude...

The Awards Evening

School one

The stage has municipal flowers and the platform party is replete with gowns. As guest of honour I shake hands with the prize winners who turn out to be those who have left for University, others with eight or more higher grades at GCSE, cups for one of each gender who excel at sports and glory under the title "Victrix or Victor Laudorum" and finally plaques for the headboy and the headgirl.

The headmaster's report is long and scripted: it dwells on the school's success against the odds which is measured by the glittering academic prizes for which the evening stands as witness.   Some blame is distributed to the Local Authority for failing to provide long needed buildings, a little to the government for not taking education seriously and a smidgeon for a few feckless parents who are responsible for the truants and disrupters. Indeed by then the subliminal message to the assembled fourth year pupils was abundantly clear........ ."You can see who we celebrate here and in your time, provided you put aside idle pursuits for the next couple of years, we shall celebrate a few of you in your turn. As for the rest of you, don't you bother us and we won't bother you. Should anyone be so foolish as to ignore those options we shall be down on you like the proverbial ton of bricks or avenging angel".

Of course no such words were actually said but neither were they necessary: there could have been no room for doubt in the discontented eyes of the grim faces amid the assembled throng as the evening wound its painful course through a violin solo to its formal vote of thanks from the bluff Chair of Governors.

School two

In the Welsh border town the awards evening was entirely different. This
school proclaimed its values and its success in a variety of powerful ways.
The citations of those we celebrated and congratulated were shared among
many members of staff who each spoke to the assembled audience of the
criteria for the selection before I shook hands with the youngsters
concerned. The evening was punctuated by dance, music and drama: the
head apologised for the fact that it was possible to have only half the school
community present but the occasion stood as proxy for an ideal which
clearly valued a wide range of human talent and achievement. Throughout,
the first year sat wide-eyed on seats at the front, clearly impressed that in
their turn they too would contribute to such an occasion.

School three

At another school in the same county, a wooden horse gazed unseeing over
the proceedings from the stage: it seemed to want to be stroked and was the
creation of a twelve year-old girl - a Grade A achievement at GCSE. As
each youngster came to the stage, the senior teacher whispered to me
something personal about their particular character and achievement and
had a smile as each experienced a mutual glance of recognition and
friendship. It spoke volumes for the school. Both occasions were long
evenings which seemed to pass in a flash as they were punctuated by fresh
occasions of interest, for example an award for "The Salt of the Earth" and
others for a variety of projects and activities sponsored by a sum from a
legacy in the name of the funding headteacher. The recipients described
what they had done with their award and we marvelled at their virtuosity.

Other schools which now resume these activities, plan yet further rites of
passage: the Chair of Governors presents gifts to retiring teachers and other
staff. Newcomers are introduced and welcomed to the assembled
community. People not of the community, but who serve it, receive special
awards. For good or ill, awards evenings are powerful occasions: they
reveal a school's value system to anyone with the eyes to see.

TWENTY QUESTIONS VISITORS MIGHT ASK ABOUT SCHOOLS AND SOME OTHER CONSIDERATIONS

1) In my first encounter with the school, are there clear signs of *welcome*: for example, on the telephone, through written signs, in the prospectus, in the entrance hall? Is the entrance clearly signed and welcoming? Do the people I meet smile and show interest in me and my purpose for visiting the school?

2) What is the state of the school corridor walls? Is there evidence of children's or other work well displayed? Are there examples of the school's achievements and do these reflect a wide range of talent - practical, sporting, artistic, dramatic, personal as well as academic?

3) Am I encouraged to see all parts of the school? As I am escorted round, do youngsters show courtesy in holding doors open, etc? Do staff talk to the students in the corridor and is most of the staff/pupil interchange of a positive, friendly nature?

4) Is there an absence of shouting and violent behaviour at break and at lunch times?

5) If I am in a classroom, what work is displayed on the wall? In a Secondary school does the display reinforce a particular subject and is there evidence of youngsters' work? In the Primary school does the work displayed show evidence of Maths, Science, Language and the Arts perhaps through a topic or a theme?

6) Am I encouraged to look at examples of children's work? Are there enthusiasm and optimism in the teachers I meet?

7) If the opportunity arises to talk to individual members of the teaching staff, encourage them to talk about pupils they teach in a particular year group: ask them to describe particular children's progress. Do they show a sensitive understanding of the individual pupil's progress to date and are they optimistic about their future development?

8) In conversation with the headteacher or a senior colleague, do they use "we" or "I"? In their description of the school's success do they include the sporting, the artistic and the personal as well as the academic?

9) Is the parents' evening to discuss pupil progress in the middle of the year when there is plenty of time left for the parent to reinforce the school's assessment with them of a youngster's progress and their strengths and weaknesses, rather than towards the end when it is too late?

10) Is there room for student and parent comments in the reporting process for youngsters' progress?

11) Do staff at the school express enthusiasm rather than disillusion for their job?

12) Are the trends for success, (eg. reading, participation in music, exams) up and failure,(eg. truancy, suspensions) down?

13) Is the school a place where staff are involved in the lunch hour and often present after school?

14) Are there plentiful opportunities for out of school activities for pupils? Can I talk with some pupils who take part? Does the school have a varied programme of visits and residential trips?

15) Do the teachers responsible for special educational need have a room (or rooms) at the heart of the school? Or are they tucked away in a hut on the edge of the school site or in other substandard accommodation?

16) Am I shown the library and is there evidence of frequent use of books? Are the microcomputers in use?

17) Ask to see the code of conduct "school rules/sanctions policies". Are they framed *positively* rather than negatively?

18) Does the school have a system of personalised letters home to comment favourably on the youngsters' progress?

19) If the school has a uniform, imagine youngsters are in normal dress...... is their behaviour still apparently cheerful and orderly? If the school has no uniform, imagine the youngsters are in uniform...... is their behaviour reasonable and perhaps less untidy than at first sight it appears?

20) Are the children of members of staff attending the school?

Some other considerations

Reading is important in all schools. The school should be able to tell you its own progress by its own indicators: it should always be up. If it is getting worse, unless there is a sudden influx of children for whom English is a second language, the school has problems. Evidence of reading successes may be shown by paired or shared reading schemes, by the use of a variety of reading methods and other schemes. There should be evidence of books and stories of the lively part of the school's life and a willingness to share the task with parents (hence paired or shared reading) together with a celebration of children who arrive at school already fluent in reading.

In **Secondary schools** the exam results are notoriously difficult to interpret. Pass rates, especially at GCSE, are very misleading for the obvious reason that a school's entry policy can affect them. Results should always be expressed as a percentage of the age group, including those who may have left before taking the exams. Analyse disparity between subjects: most schools now use a computer software program to analyse the performance of the same children in different subjects. As with all performance indicators, successful schools are always comparing the data over time, for example 2, 3, 4, 5, even more years, to reveal an ever upward trend.

They will try to compare the speed of that upward trend with any comparable trend, locally or nationally, in order to satisfy themselves that they are improving, at the very least, at a speed comparable with others, even if of course there is no point in comparing the actual performance with schools which are in very different circumstances.

In **all** successful primary and secondary schools, data, similarly comparing the present with the school's own previous performance and affecting attendance and staff turnover, are collected and analysed in order that some fine tuning of existing practices can take place in order to improve the successful outcomes for staff and students alike.

Tailpiece...

Final Thoughts

At the very beginning of this book I created an image of 'words and tune' for the successful school. In a sense, what each chapter has been designed to do is to rehearse the general approach to *leadership*, to *collective review*, to *staff development*, to the *climate* of schooling, to the *organisation* of school life and it has even touched on the most important issue of all, *teaching and learning* itself.

Perhaps it has all been painfully obvious. Just conceivably however at a few points, for each reader, there may have been a nod of assent to issues subconsciously assumed and half-forgotten. I hope that there will be points with which people will disagree. Will that lead readers to a new critical approach to an issue at their school? Of course, perhaps too there will be matters on which readers thinks I am plain daft, even dangerously wrong. If so I hope I shall hear from you.

And yet..... there remains the question of *melody, harmony* and *tune*. I have reread what is written and confess that I catch only a snatch of the melody of successful schooling. Perhaps our research project, mentioned right at the beginning, will get us closer. I can imagine the conscientious, eager, hard-working systems analyst reading the book and noting the patterns and the steps to take grimly determined, kitted out as it were with a mental clipboard, to put it all into practice and wondering subsequently why it didn't work and worse still, perhaps not even noticing that it didn't!

There is at the heart of successful teaching and schooling an *elusive* factor. For me it is encapsulated in the comment of a fifteen year-old girl. Sharon was one of a group of young truants or school misfits, who were suspended from their school and met irregularly with professionals from the support services from time to time. On my second visit, when the giggling and display had subsided, Sharon identified a teacher as a good one, not because he was strict, nor because he was liberal but because "he was interested in you and you knew it by what he did, not by what he said".

How do you make that more rather than less likely in the school? Is it by paying attention to the social cement of the staff as well as of the youngsters? In other words if the school play, the residential trip.....the musical, sporting and extra-curricular activities are important for the children and their relationships with the staff, is something similar needed for staff? If so can that be planned or does it happen as a result of other factors? Is it perhaps a group of young staff who reinvigorate a school, not merely by their deeds in the school but by their social energy as a group? Do those staffrooms which have accumulated social idiosyncrasies that remember birthdays, celebrate each others' successes and find it possible to laugh and cry together, make for good schooling? How are they created? Is it in the unpredictable thoughtfulness of senior colleagues who show they care? Is it the unexpected praise? Is it the celebration of an accumulated string of past successes which each and every member of staff knows must grow ever longer with each year and to which they personally want to contribute? And is all that achieved through care in appointments?

Whatever it is, I am utterly convinced that therein lies more of the tune. I hope this book has encouraged the reader to recall or recognise a few more bars of the tune. *If you have, my colleagues and I would like to hear from you.* Certainly we promise to be back in a couple of years with a lot more to say, based on hard evidence from schools which have opened their practices to our critical but positive gaze.

APPENDIX   A Selected List of References

Powell R (1990). Resources for Flexible Learning. Network Educational Press.

Waterhouse P (1990). Classroom Management. Network Educational Press.

Waterhouse P (1990). Flexible Learning: An Outline. Network Educational Press.

Waterhouse P (1990). Tutoring. Network Educational Press.

Research into effective schooling

Research in the 1980s has demonstrated that some schools at both primary and secondary level, are more effective than others in terms of helping pupils to progress academically and in related objectives. The research is less successful in demonstrating *why* some schools are more effective than others and exactly *which* factors are related to positive school effects. Those who wish to start the quest for more information should look at:

Gray J (1990). The Quality of Schooling: Frameworks for Judgement. In British Journal of Education Studies Vol. 38 No. 3 (August).

Mortimore P et al (1988).   School Matters - The Junior Years. Open Books.

Reid K, Hopkins D, and **Holly K** (1987). Towards the Effective School. Oxford: Blackwell.

Rutter M et al (1979). Fifteen Thousand Hours: Secondary Schools and their Effect on Children. Open Books.

Sanday A (1990). Making Schools More Effective. Warwick University.

Smith D and **Tomlinson S** (1990). The School Effect. PSI

Tizard B et al (1988). Young Children at School in the Inner City. Lawrence Erlbaum.

Tomlinson J (1990).   Small, Rural and Effective. Warwick University.

The Teaching and Learning Series

This book, *What Makes a Good School?* is the fifth in the series and is closely related to four others which examine important issues both for the classroom teacher and the school or college manager.

Book 1, *Flexible Learning: an Outline*, by **Philip Waterhouse** provides an outline of all the key questions in the debate on teaching and learning styles. He examines the rationale, contexts and methods of *flexible learning*:

- The National Curriculum
- Assessment
- TVEI
- Records of Achievement
- Study skills

- Tutoring
- The flexible use of space, time, money and people
- The use of libraries and resource centres

Flexible Learning: an Outline is a **handbook**. Each chapter provides an agenda, a checklist of key issues and will be invaluable to all those interested in stimulating discussion or raising awareness on the subject of how teachers teach and how students learn.

ISBN 1 85539 003 5 £6.50

Book 2, *Classroom Management*, by **Philip Waterhouse**, provides a detailed insight into the management of a wide variety of teaching and learning strategies. It provides practical advice on:

- Planning and organisation of schemes of work
- Differentiation
- Assignments
- Management of resources
- The organisation and layout of classrooms
- Assessment and recording
- Managing the whole class, small group and individual work.

The book will be a valuable handbook for both classroom teachers and for those managing teaching and learning in schools and colleges.

ISBN 1 85539 004 3 £6.50

Book 3, *Resources for Flexible Learning,* by **Robert Powell**, provides practical advice on the complex question of resources.

- Defining flexible resources
- Choosing and evaluating resources
- Adapting existing materials
- Making full use of libraries / resource centres
- Preparing study guides
- Thinking about design and layout
- Using desktop publishing.

The book will suggest ways in which teachers and students can use a wide variety of resources both to satisfy the demands of the National Curriculum and to develop independent learning skills.

ISBN 1 85539 005 1 £6.50

Book 4, *Tutoring,* by **Philip Waterhouse** explores the possibilities of skilful tutoring. It presents clearly:

- The rationale and objectives of tutoring
- The contexts for tutoring
- Arrangements for tutoring
- Tutoring styles
- Tutoring techniques.

The book will serve as an invaluable handbook for all those in schools and colleges seeking to provide guidance and support to students both in the classroom and in more informal learning situations.

ISBN 1 85539 006 X £6.50

All books in the *Teaching and Learning Series* £4.50. Discounts available for bulk orders direct from the publishers. Order forms and further details from:

Network Educational Press, PO Box 635, Stafford ST17 0JR.

Telephone: 0785 225515

Other Titles from Network Educational Press

Coursework Enquiry/Study Guides
introduced by **Philip Waterhouse**

A series of photocopiable coursework enquiry/study guides is available in the following subject areas:

☐ Geography ☐ Humanities ☐ Business Studies

Each subject pack contains 30 different enquiries on a wide range of topics. The guides provide:

- clear, practical guidance
- advice on resources, activities and presentation
- scope for individual, group or class investigations
- flexibility in use.

90,000 of these guides have purchased by schools and colleges since their publication in May 1989. (The Geography pack was awarded the title **Best Secondary Text 1989** by the Geography Association.) The guides have been used in:

- Geography, Humanities and Business Studies (13-16)
- English (13-16)
- General Studies and PSE (14-18)
- CPVE and B TEC (16+).

Each pack £35.00. A full set of Geography, Humanities and Business Studies £95.00. Brochures and order forms from the publishers.

Forthcoming Titles

The success of the study guides has led us to increase the range of subjects. During Spring 1992, guides will be published in:

☐ Technology (from a range of disciplines) ☐ English Language

☐ Science

☐ History ☐ Modern Languages

Details of all these publications from:

Network Educational Press, PO Box 635, Stafford ST17 0JR

Telephone: 0785 225515

English Literature

Activities / Assignments Guides

A series of photocopiable guides which support flexible styles of teaching and learning in English Literature.

□   **16 titles in the range**

The guides provide a fresh and imaginative approach to English Literature and will appeal to:

- experienced teachers looking for new ideas
- teachers new to particular texts
- student teachers
- non-specialist teachers of English.

Each guide has three sections:

- a summary of key plot events (for easy reference)
- a collection of varied learning activities
- a collection of assignments.

The activities seek to develop a wide range of student skills:

- oral skills
- paired and small group work
- improvisation and role play
- discursive, narrative and creative writing.

The assignments engage the student in a detailed study of the text, are clearly differentiated, and seek to provide:

- a critical understanding of plot, character, and style
- suggestions for the open study or extension work
- scope for independent research
- coursework opportunities in English.

To be published Summer Term 1991 £30.00 per photocopiable pack of 16 titles. Available from the publishers:

**Network Educational Press, PO Box 635, Stafford ST17 0JR
Telephone: 0785 225515**